what are the rules?

Player 1 starts first. player 1 reads the questions aloud and chooses an answer in the silliest and wackiest way possible. if the reason makes player 2 laugh, then player 1 scores point. Take turns going back and forth, and write down the score at the end of each round.

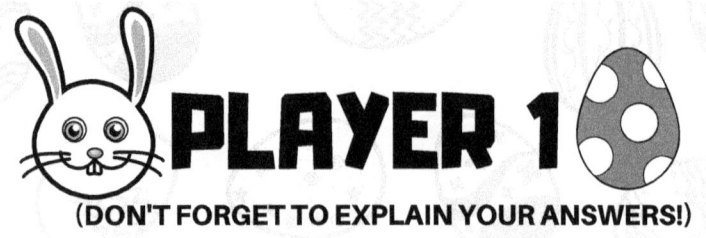
PLAYER 1
(DON'T FORGET TO EXPLAIN YOUR ANSWERS!)

Would you rather ride on the Easter Bunny's back
or
swing from his long ears?

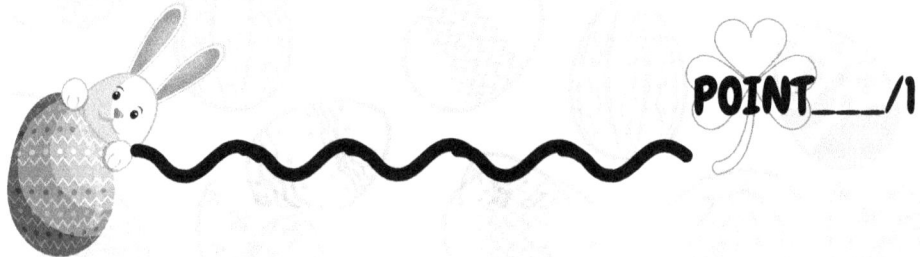

POINT___/1

Would you rather hide the Easter eggs
or
hunt for the Easter eggs?

POINT___/1

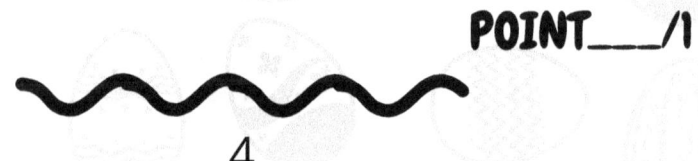

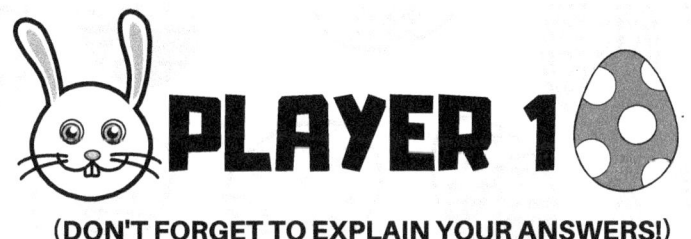

PLAYER 1

(DON'T FORGET TO EXPLAIN YOUR ANSWERS!)

Would you rather share your Easter chocolates with your friends or keep them all to yourself?

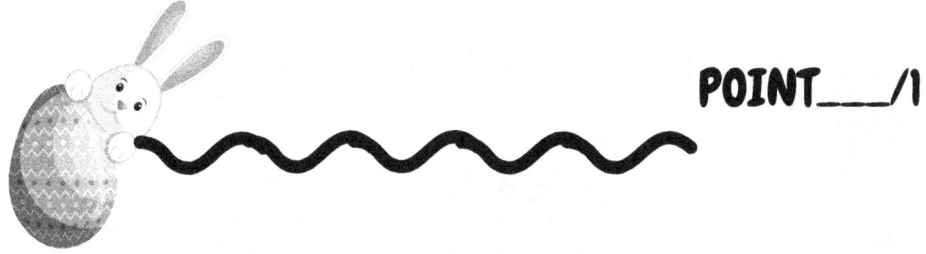

POINT___/1

Would you rather be best friends with the Easter Bunny or Santa Claus?

POINT___/1

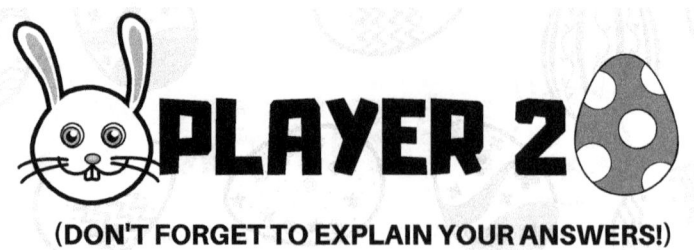

PLAYER 2

(DON'T FORGET TO EXPLAIN YOUR ANSWERS!)

Would you rather spend the day with the Easter Bunny
or
the Tooth Fairy?

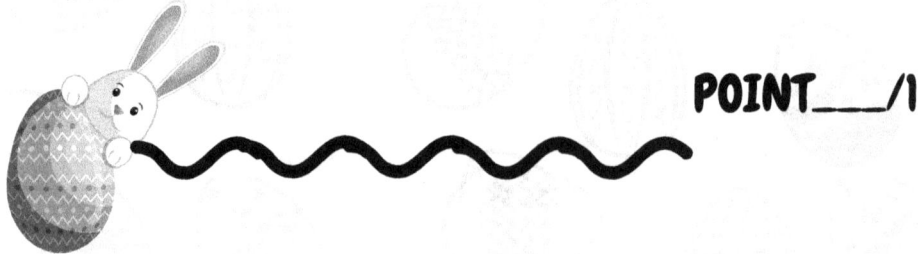

POINT____/1

Would you rather search for Easter eggs at the bottom of the ocean
or
on the top of a mountain?

POINT____/1

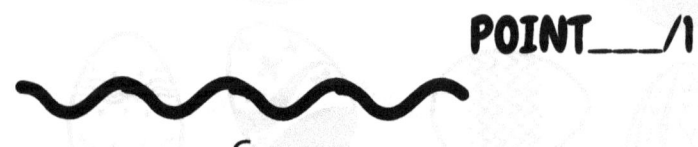

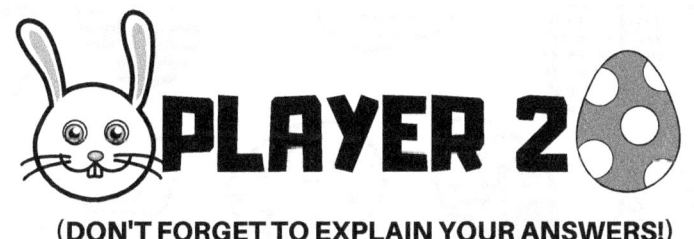

(DON'T FORGET TO EXPLAIN YOUR ANSWERS!)

Would you rather decorate 100 Easter eggs or decorate 100 Easter cookies?

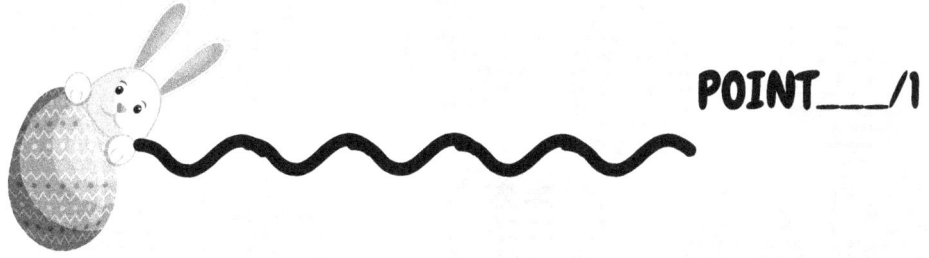

POINT____/1

Would you rather eat a GIANT chocolate bunny or a GIANT jelly bean?

POINT____/1

PLAYER 1 POINT___/4

PLAYER 2 POINT___/4

(DON'T FORGET TO EXPLAIN YOUR ANSWERS!)

Would you rather visit Santa, at the North Pole
or, visit the Easter Bunny?or inside?

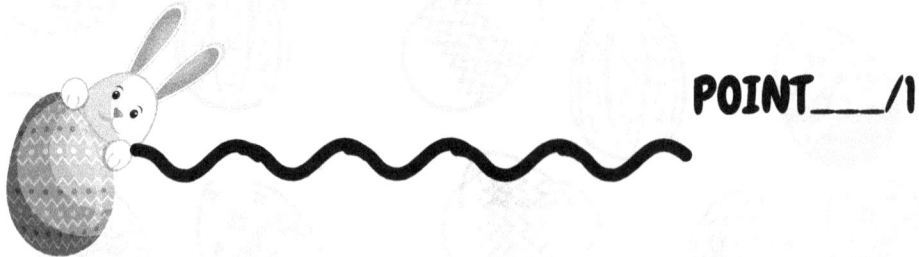

POINT___/1

Would you rather hunt for Easter eggs outside
or
inside?

POINT___/1

PLAYER 1

(DON'T FORGET TO EXPLAIN YOUR ANSWERS!)

Would you rather receive one BIG chocolate egg
or
50 small chocolate eggs?

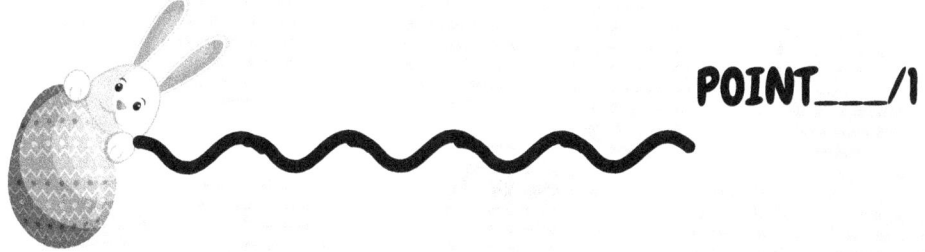

POINT___/1

Would you rather eat only chocolate eggs for 6 months
or
eat only hard-boiled eggs for 6 months?

POINT___/1

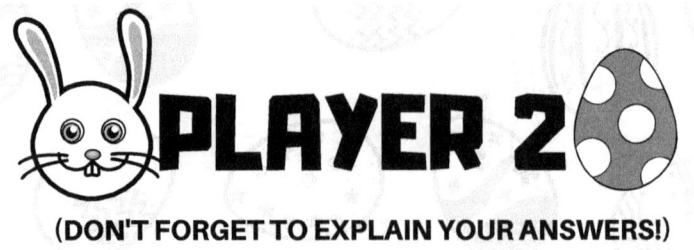

PLAYER 2

(DON'T FORGET TO EXPLAIN YOUR ANSWERS!)

Would you rather wear a bunny costume in gym class
or
wear a Santa suit in gym class?

POINT____/1

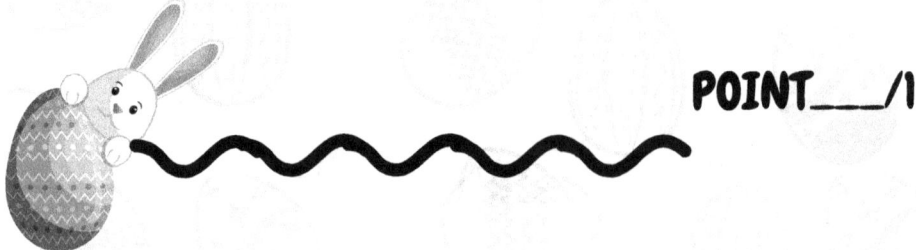

Would you rather visit a chocolate factory
or
a candy factory?

POINT____/1

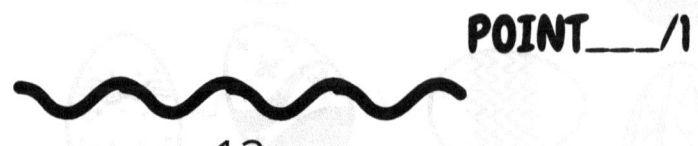

12

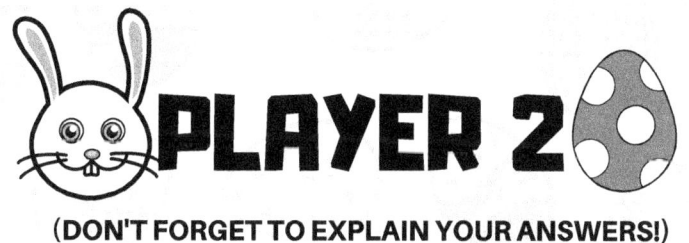

PLAYER 2

(DON'T FORGET TO EXPLAIN YOUR ANSWERS!)

Would you rather hide the Easter eggs
or
hunt for the Easter eggs?

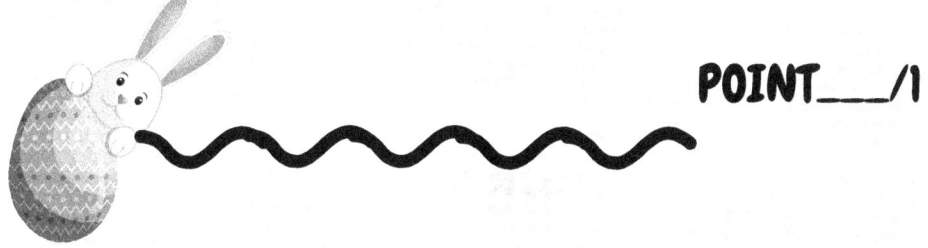

POINT___/1

Would you rather eat only carrots for a month
or
only chocolate for a month?

POINT___/1

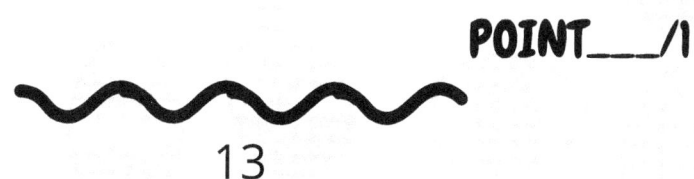

PLAYER 1 POINT___/4

PLAYER 2 POINT___/4

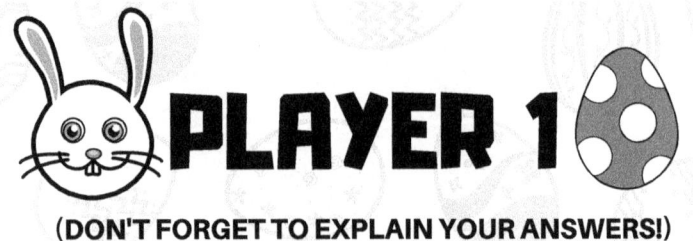
PLAYER 1

(DON'T FORGET TO EXPLAIN YOUR ANSWERS!)

Would you rather have BIG bunny ears
or
a fluffy bunny tail?

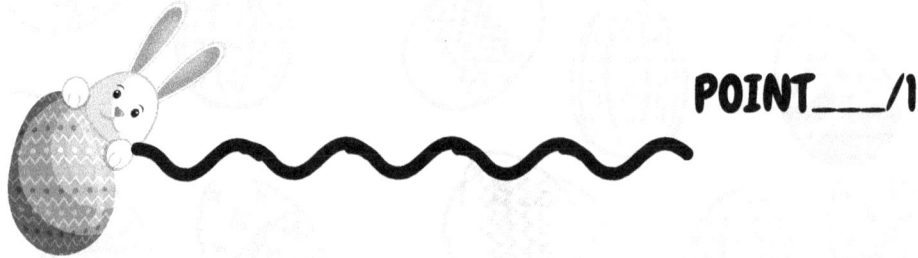

POINT____/1

Would you rather have an extra week of March Break
or
an extra 10 chocolate bunnies?

POINT____/1

PLAYER 1

(DON'T FORGET TO EXPLAIN YOUR ANSWERS!)

Would you rather receive Easter candy from your teacher
or
have no homework for a day?

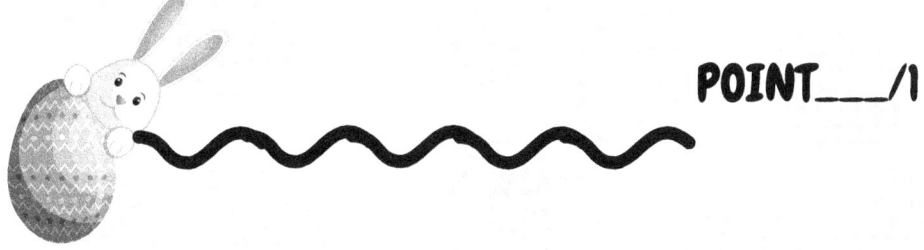

POINT___/1

Would you rather have to wear a suit of plastic Easter eggs
or
a suit of Peeps all day?

POINT___/1

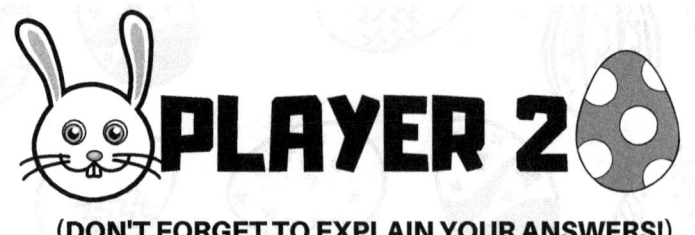

PLAYER 2

(DON'T FORGET TO EXPLAIN YOUR ANSWERS!)

Would you rather be able to say "Happy Easter" in 100 languages or know the answer to 1000 random trivia questions?

POINT____/1

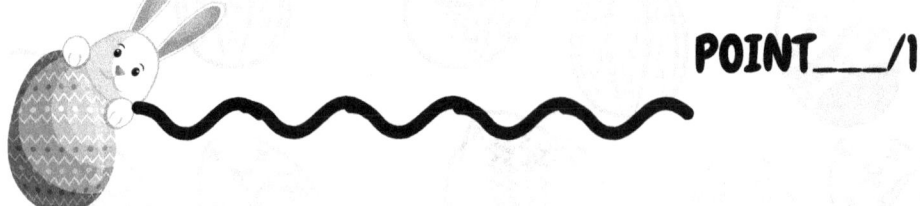

Would you rather eat ham for Easter dinner or lamb?

POINT____/1

PLAYER 2

(DON'T FORGET TO EXPLAIN YOUR ANSWERS!)

Would you rather have to wear a jellybeans stuck in your teeth all day,
or
walk around with a chocolate moustache?

POINT___/1

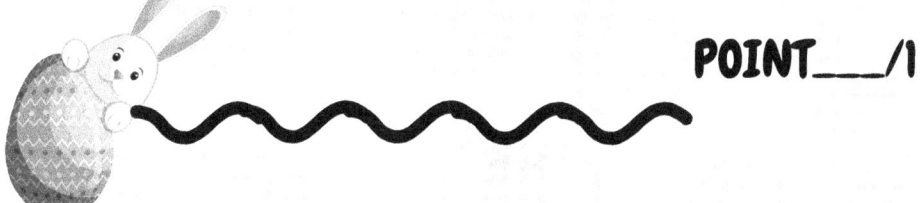

Would you rather have to start every sentence by kissing an Easter egg first
or
sing everything you say on Easter?

POINT___/1

PLAYER 1 POINT___/4

PLAYER 2 POINT___/4

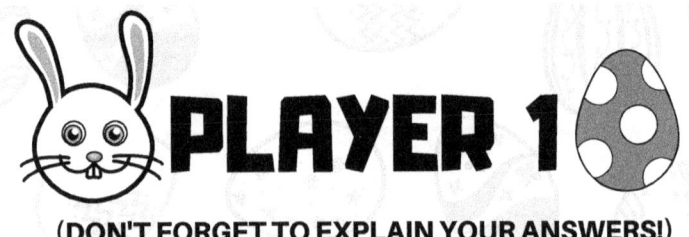
PLAYER 1
(DON'T FORGET TO EXPLAIN YOUR ANSWERS!)

Would you rather spend Easter in a home with no Internet
or
a home without indoor plumbing?

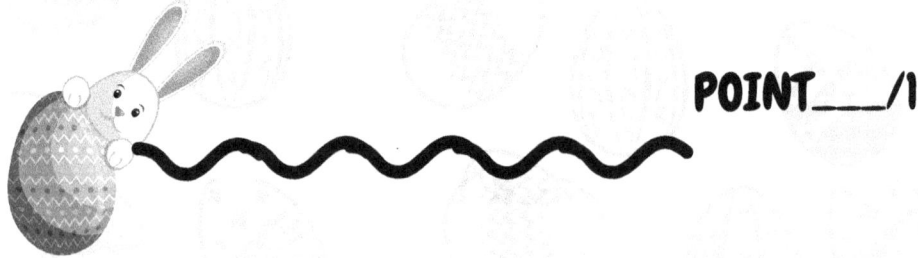

POINT___/1

Would you rather have snow on Easter
or
a warm 80-degree day?

POINT___/1

22

PLAYER 1

(DON'T FORGET TO EXPLAIN YOUR ANSWERS!)

Would you rather have to wear your shoes on the wrong feet for Easter
or
wear your pants backwards?

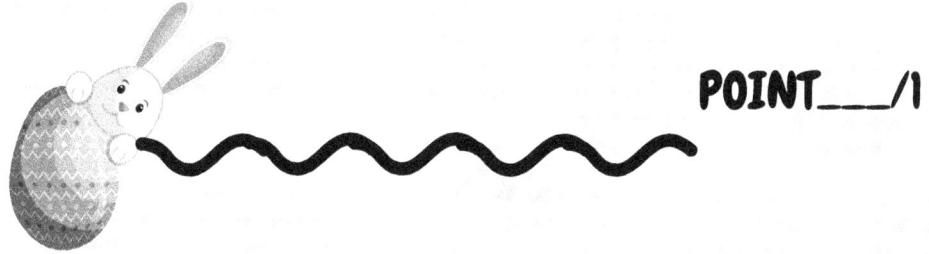

POINT____/1

Would you rather have to unwrap 1000 pieces of foil-wrapped chocolate eggs
or
pop 1000 pastel colored balloons?

POINT____/1

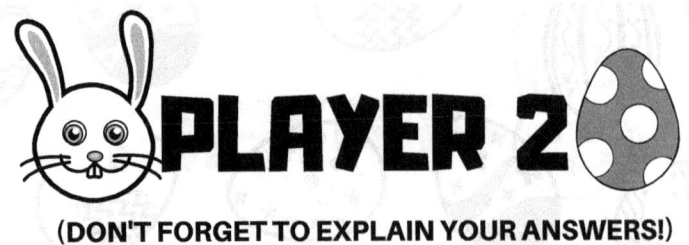

PLAYER 2

(DON'T FORGET TO EXPLAIN YOUR ANSWERS!)

Would you rather have to receive a kiss on the lips from a llama or a lick on the face from a pig?

POINT___/1

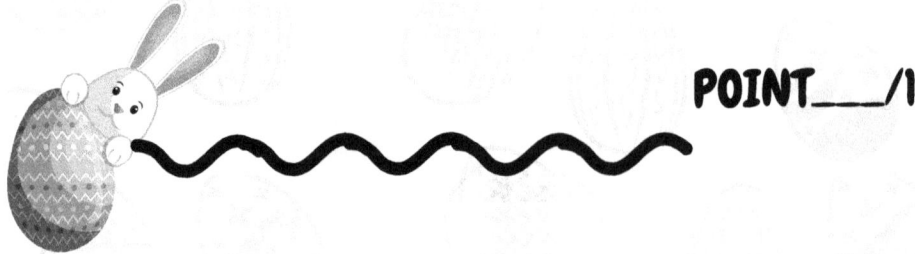

Would you rather eat 12 chocolate eggs or 12 marshmallow Peeps?

POINT___/1

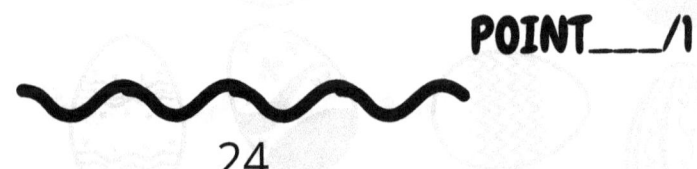

PLAYER 2
(DON'T FORGET TO EXPLAIN YOUR ANSWERS!)

Would you rather spend Easter with the ability to be invisible
or
have the ability to fly?

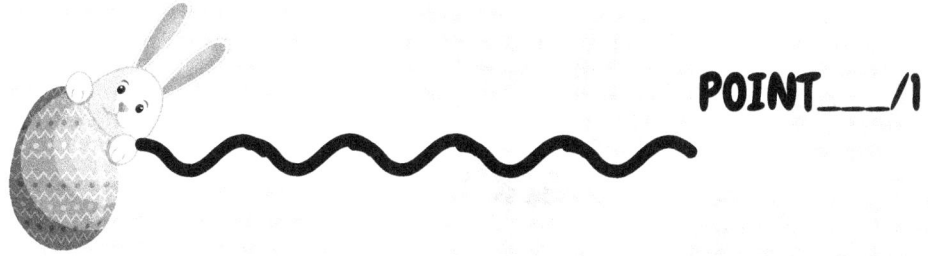

POINT___/1

Would you rather eat 3 chocolate covered dog biscuits
or
the greens from 3 carrots?

POINT___/1

PLAYER 1 POINT___/4

PLAYER 2 POINT___/4

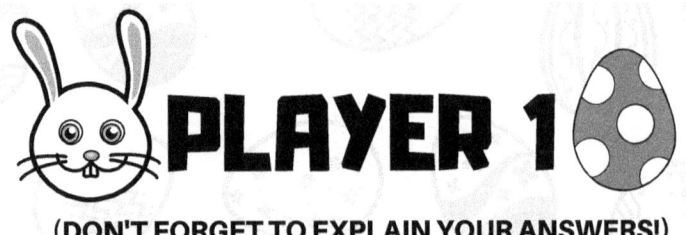

PLAYER 1

(DON'T FORGET TO EXPLAIN YOUR ANSWERS!)

Would you rather receive a dozen carrots
or
a dozen chocolate eggs on Valentine's Day?

POINT___/1

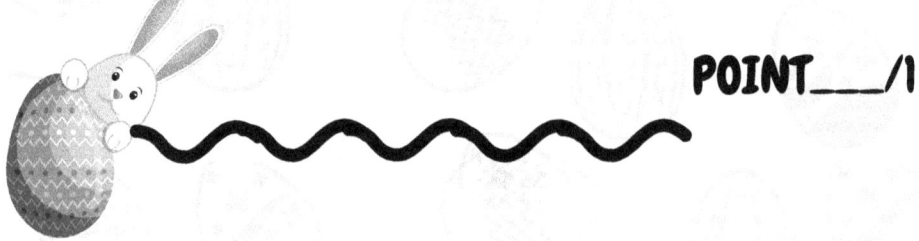

Would you rather have flowers grow in your footsteps
or
confetti fall from the sky every time you sit down?

POINT___/1

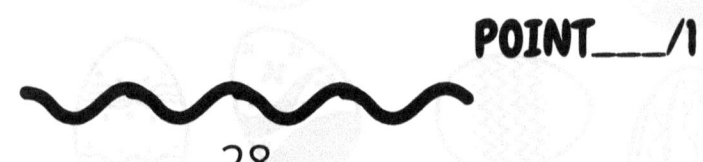

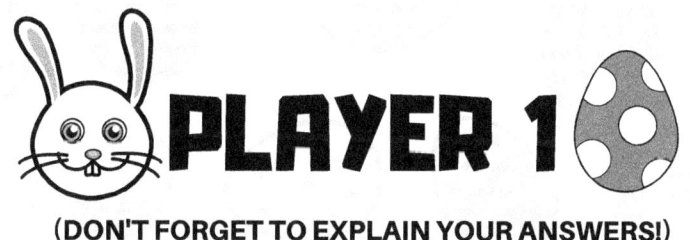

PLAYER 1

(DON'T FORGET TO EXPLAIN YOUR ANSWERS!)

Would you rather have to say everything you are thinking
or
never be able to speak on Easter?

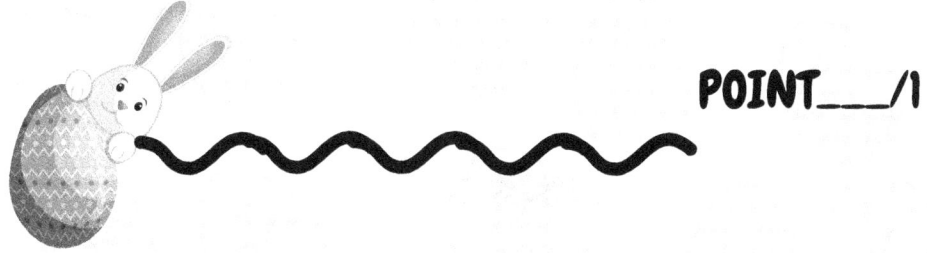

POINT___/1

Would you rather have to eat 12 chocolate covered earthworms on Easter
or
12 spicy hot peppers?

POINT___/1

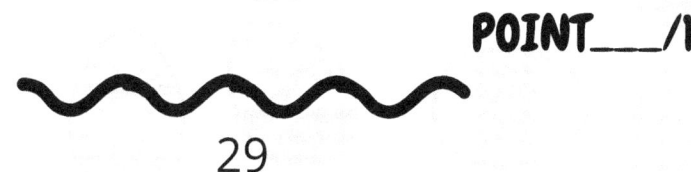

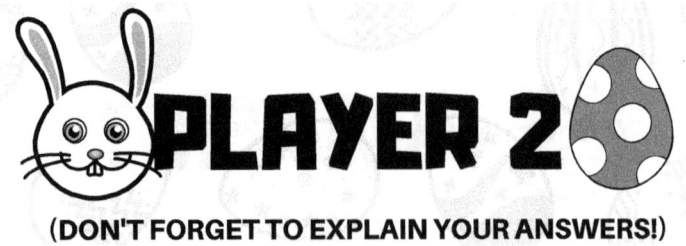
PLAYER 2

(DON'T FORGET TO EXPLAIN YOUR ANSWERS!)

Would you rather have to eat an entire 5 lb. chocolate bunny
or
a drink a gallon of red punch?

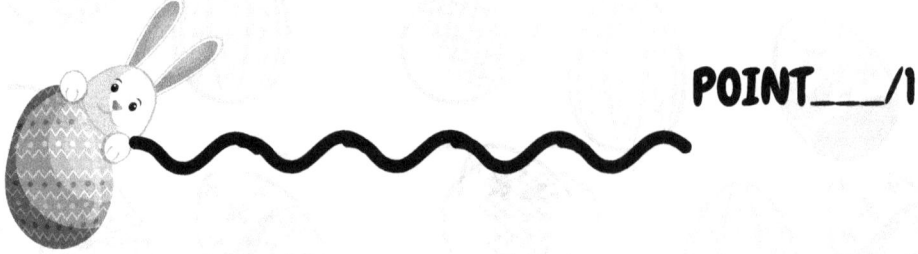

POINT___/1

Would you rather have to kiss your dog on the lips
or
your least favorite teacher on the cheek for Easter?

POINT___/1

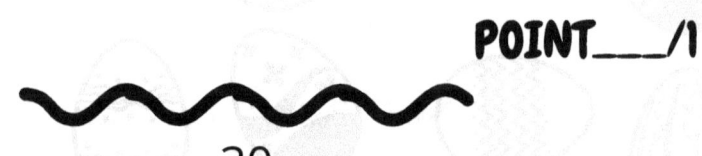

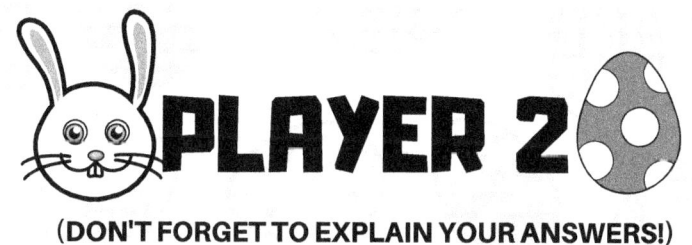

PLAYER 2

(DON'T FORGET TO EXPLAIN YOUR ANSWERS!)

Would you rather have Peeps stuck in your hair
or
jellybeans stuck to your teeth?

POINT___/1

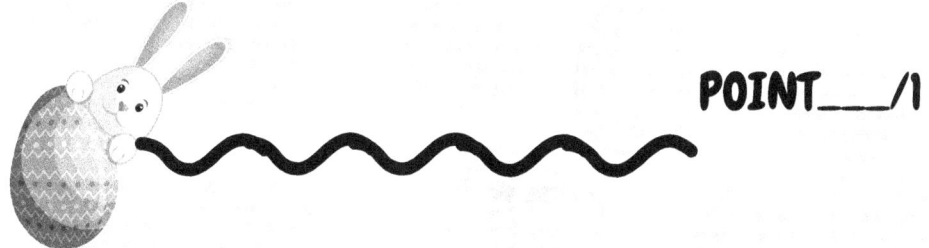

Would you rather have to whisper "Happy Easter" in your math teacher's ear
or
shout "Happy Easter" at the gym teacher?

POINT___/1

PLAYER 1 POINT___/4

PLAYER 2 POINT___/4

PLAYER 1

(DON'T FORGET TO EXPLAIN YOUR ANSWERS!)

Would you rather have to wear a giant bunny costume
or
a giant Easter egg costume?

POINT___/1

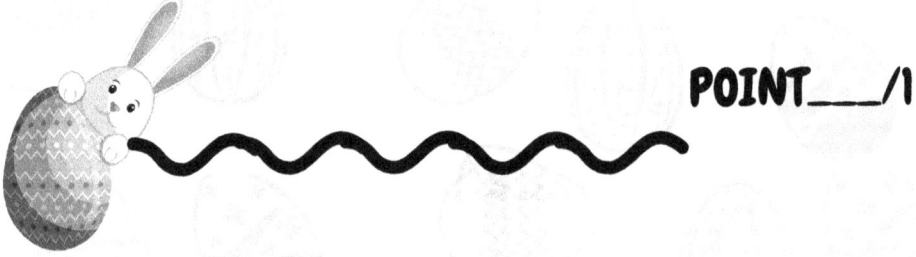

Would you rather be allergic to grass
or
allergic to chocolate?

POINT___/1

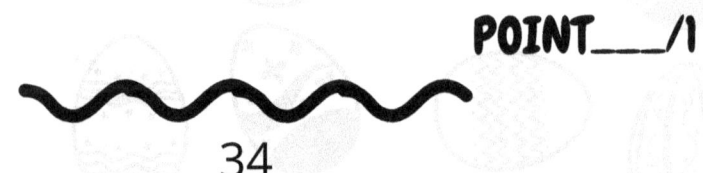

PLAYER 1

(DON'T FORGET TO EXPLAIN YOUR ANSWERS!)

Would you rather wear a shirt tomorrow that lists all of the things you did on Easter
or
all of the candy you ate?

POINT____/1

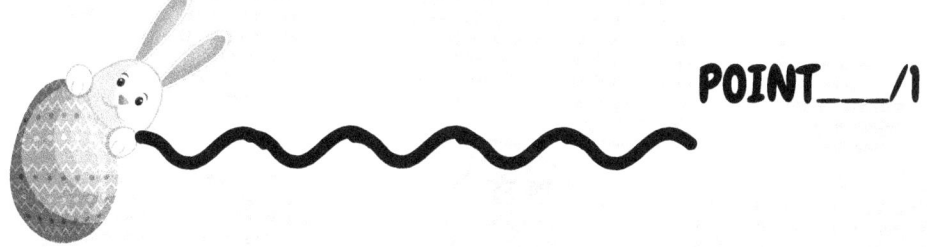

Would you rather be stuck in a home that has no power on Easter
or
one that has no food?

POINT____/1

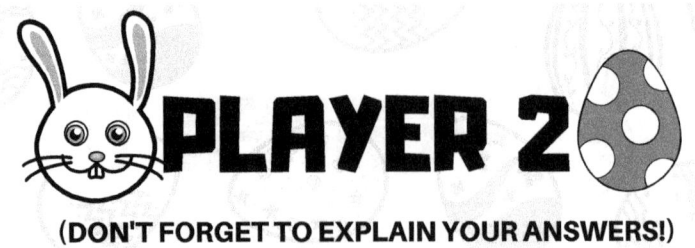

PLAYER 2

(DON'T FORGET TO EXPLAIN YOUR ANSWERS!)

Would you rather have Easter grass for hair
or
teeth shaped like Peeps?

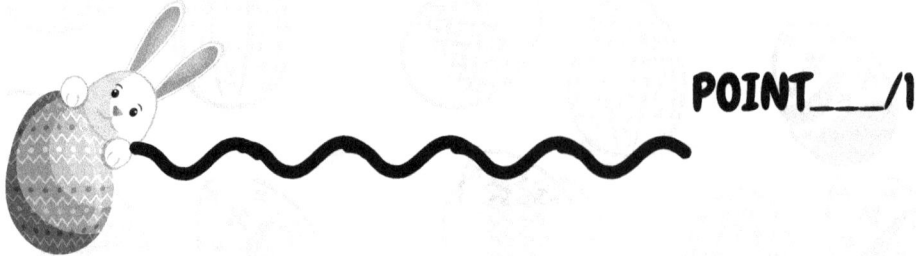

POINT____/1

Would you rather swim in a pool of Easter punch
or
a pool of warm cocoa?

POINT____/1

PLAYER 2

(DON'T FORGET TO EXPLAIN YOUR ANSWERS!)

Would you rather be invited to the White House to celebrate Easter
or
have a celebrity chef come to your house to make your Easter dinner?

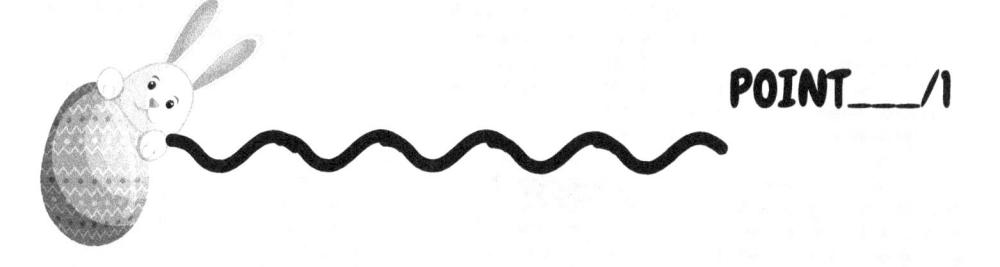

POINT___/1

Would you rather receive a live chick for Easter
or
a chocolate bunny?

POINT___/1

PLAYER 1 POINT___/4

PLAYER 2 POINT___/4

ROUND 6

PLAYER 1

(DON'T FORGET TO EXPLAIN YOUR ANSWERS!)

Would you rather be forced to hang out with someone you don't like on Easter
or
have your siblings follow you around in school all week after Spring Break?

POINT____/1

Would you rather have a constant itch
or
constant hiccups on Easter?

POINT____/1

PLAYER 1

(DON'T FORGET TO EXPLAIN YOUR ANSWERS!)

Would you rather stroke a friendly lion that's awake
or
stroke an unfriendly lion while it's asleep?

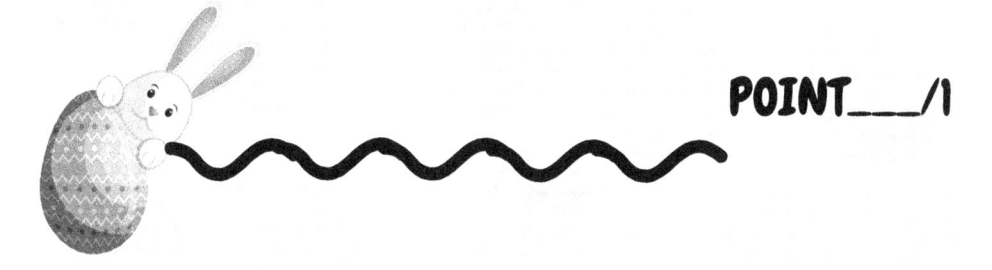

POINT___/1

Would you rather have to go through Spring Break wearing earplugs
or
nose plugs?

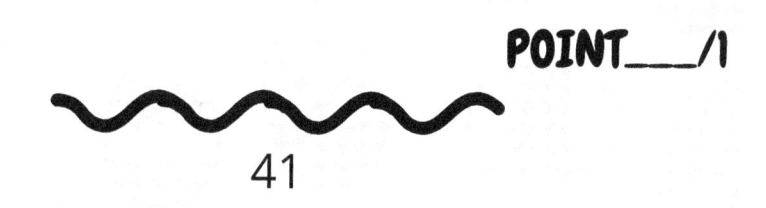

POINT___/1

PLAYER 2

(DON'T FORGET TO EXPLAIN YOUR ANSWERS!)

Would you rather have to eat 100 chocolate bunnies on Easter
or
never eat chocolate again?

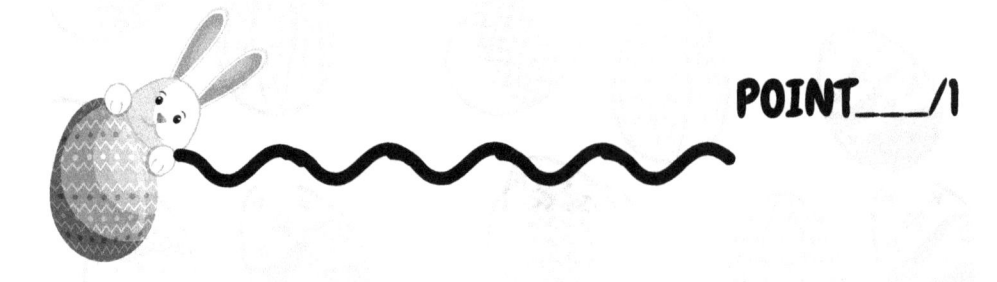

POINT___/1

Would you rather eat your fingernails
or
eat your toenails?

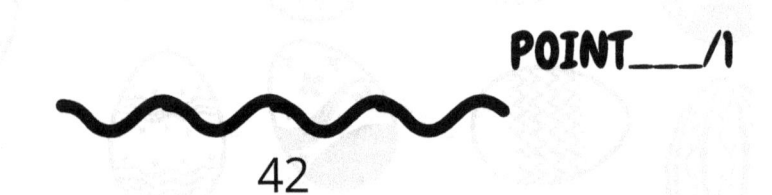

POINT___/1

PLAYER 2

(DON'T FORGET TO EXPLAIN YOUR ANSWERS!)

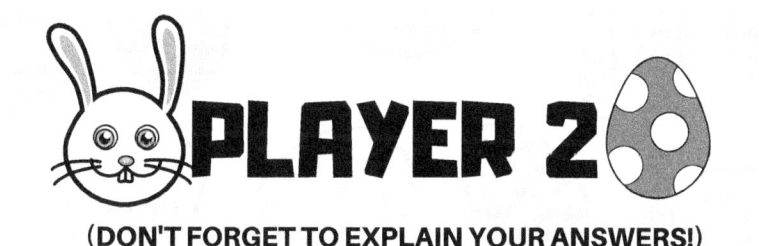

Would you rather have to read a page from your diary in front of the class before Spring Break
or
share a video of your most embarrassing moment?

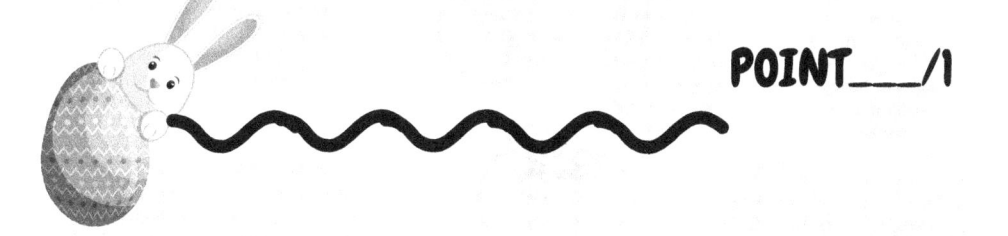

POINT___/1

Would you rather sound like an old person
or
look like an old person?

POINT___/1

PLAYER 1 POINT___/4

PLAYER 2 POINT___/4

ROUND 6

PLAYER 1

(DON'T FORGET TO EXPLAIN YOUR ANSWERS!)

Would you rather have ears shaped like a bunny's ears
or
a beak like a baby chick?

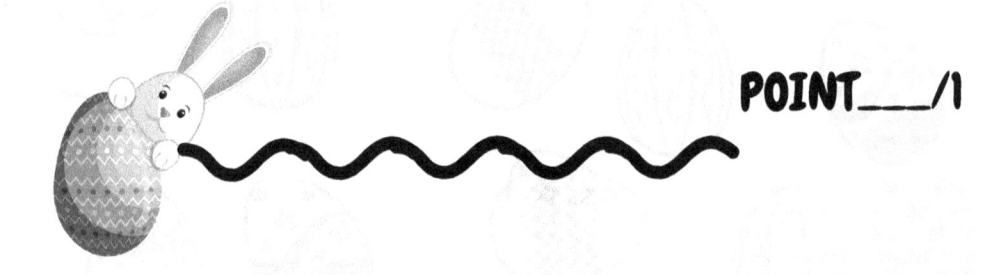

POINT____/1

Would you rather have a really fat tummy
or
a tummy that makes rumbling noises a lot?

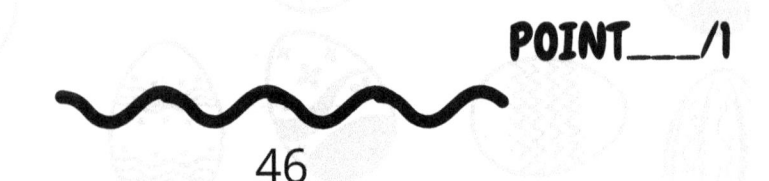

POINT____/1

46

PLAYER 1

(DON'T FORGET TO EXPLAIN YOUR ANSWERS!)

Would you rather sit on something really wet
or
sit on something really cold?

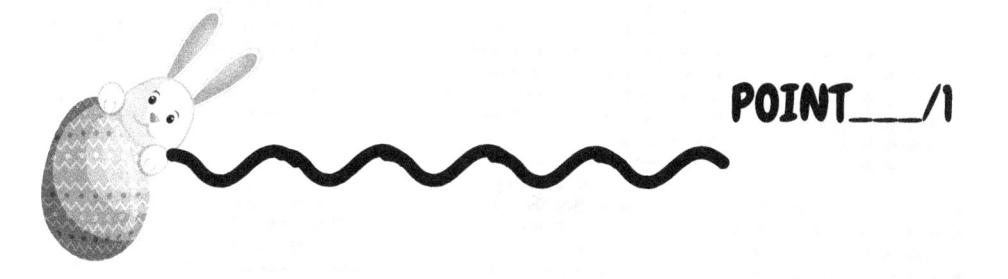

POINT___/1

Would you rather be able to travel through time on Easter
or
have the ability to read minds?

POINT___/1

PLAYER 2

(DON'T FORGET TO EXPLAIN YOUR ANSWERS!)

Would you rather scream while watching a scary movie
or
pee in your pants while watching a scary movie?

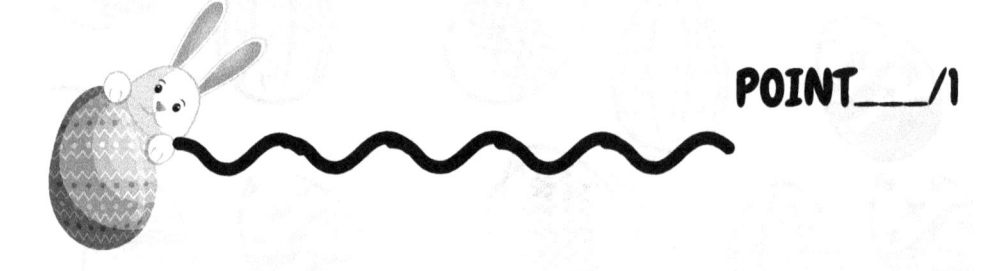

POINT____/1

Would you rather have to kiss a toad
or
lick your best friend's big toe on Easter?

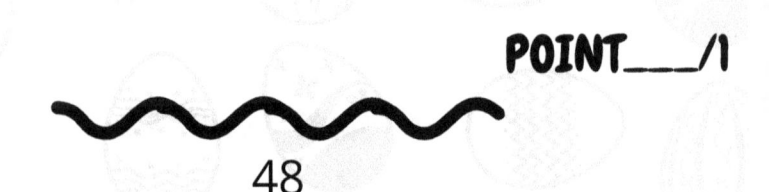

POINT____/1

PLAYER 2

(DON'T FORGET TO EXPLAIN YOUR ANSWERS!)

Would you rather fall asleep in class
or
fall asleep on the bus?

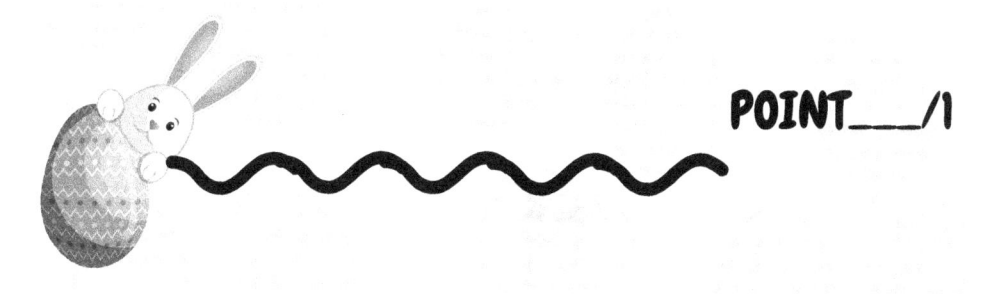

POINT___/1

Would you rather kiss a frog
or
hug a porcupine on Easter?

POINT___/1

PLAYER 1 POINT___/4

PLAYER 2 POINT___/4

ROUND 6

PLAYER 1

(DON'T FORGET TO EXPLAIN YOUR ANSWERS!)

Would you rather have to sing Bruno Mars' "Just the Way You Are" on a YouTube video that everyone you know will see

or

appear in Diet Coke commercial on TV dressed as the Easter Bunny?

POINT___/1

Would you rather wear dirty clothes for a week

or

wear the same outfit every day for a week?

POINT___/1

PLAYER 1

(DON'T FORGET TO EXPLAIN YOUR ANSWERS!)

Would you rather forget to take your toothbrush for a sleepover
or
forget to take your towel for a sleepover?

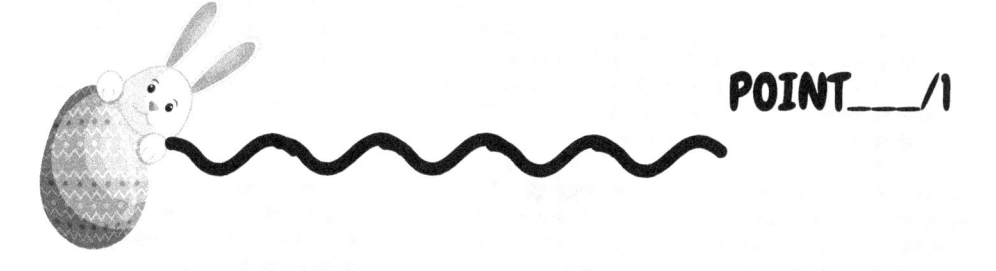

POINT___/1

Would you rather have to spend the next week dressed as the Easter Bunny
or
have to find 500 jellybeans hidden on the lawn?

POINT___/1

PLAYER 2

(DON'T FORGET TO EXPLAIN YOUR ANSWERS!)

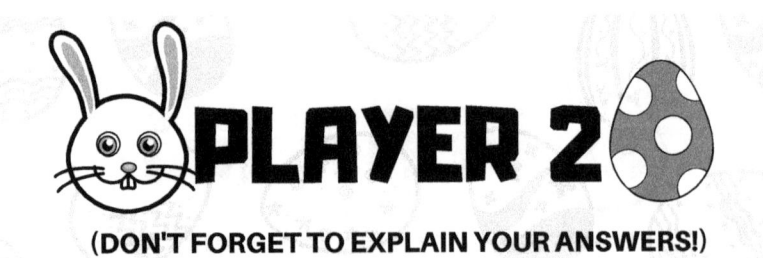

Would you rather have to sign all of your homework with "XOXOXOXO"
or
have to wear a red lipstick kiss on your cheek the day after Spring Break?

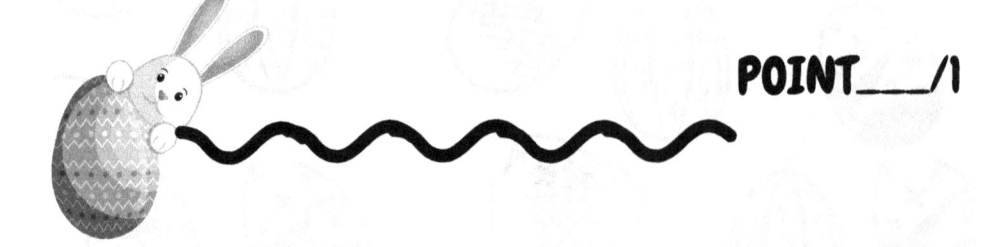

POINT____/1

Would you rather have a toy that walks
or
a toy that talks?

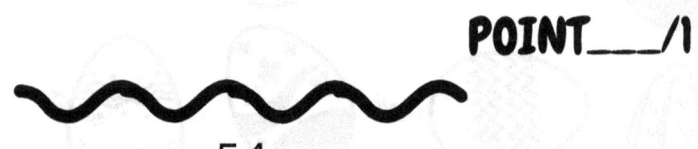

POINT____/1

PLAYER 2

(DON'T FORGET TO EXPLAIN YOUR ANSWERS!)

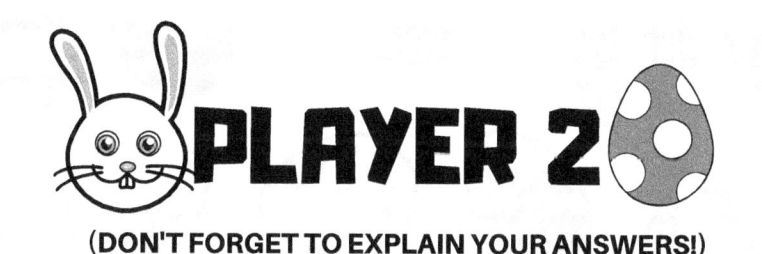

Would you rather eat a year's worth of pizza in one night
or
never eat pizza again?

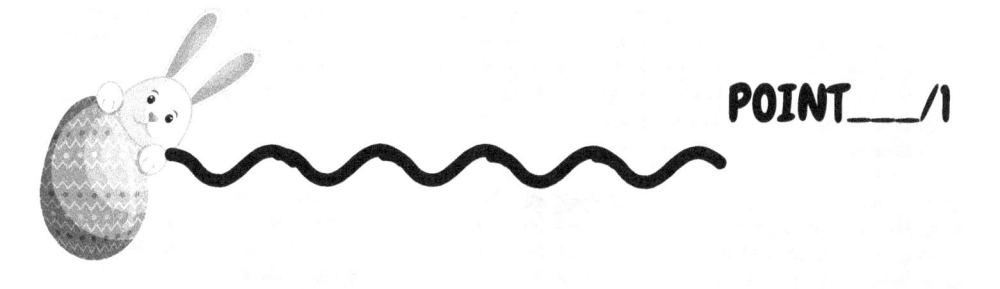

POINT____/1

Would you rather have to go without TV and Internet on Easter
or
without candy?

POINT____/1

PLAYER 1 POINT___/4

PLAYER 2 POINT___/4

ROUND 7

PLAYER 1

(DON'T FORGET TO EXPLAIN YOUR ANSWERS!)

Would you rather have to eat a Easter dinner prepared by your dog
or
have to drink a gallon of ketchup?

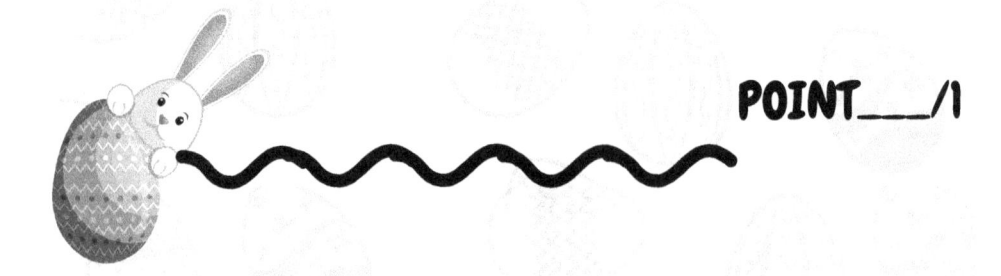

POINT___/1

Would you rather be able to talk to animals
or
be able to be an animal of your choice?

POINT___/1

PLAYER 1

(DON'T FORGET TO EXPLAIN YOUR ANSWERS!)

Would you rather have milk run down your nose every time you laugh
or
have milk run out of your eyes every time you cried?

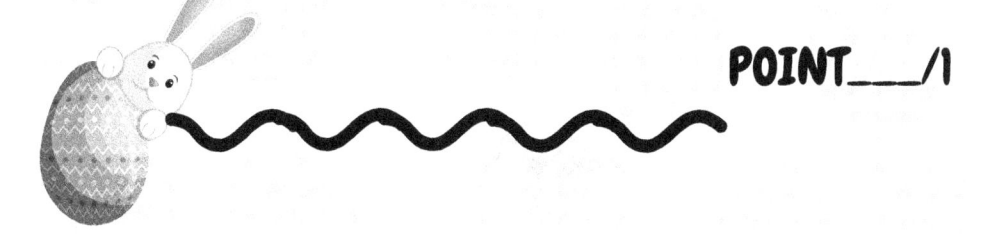

POINT___/1

Would you rather own a bunny that can talk
or
a chick that can lay chocolare eggs?

POINT___/1

PLAYER 2

(DON'T FORGET TO EXPLAIN YOUR ANSWERS!)

Would you rather have gum stuck to the bottom of your shoe
or
tissue paper stuck to the bottom of your shoe?

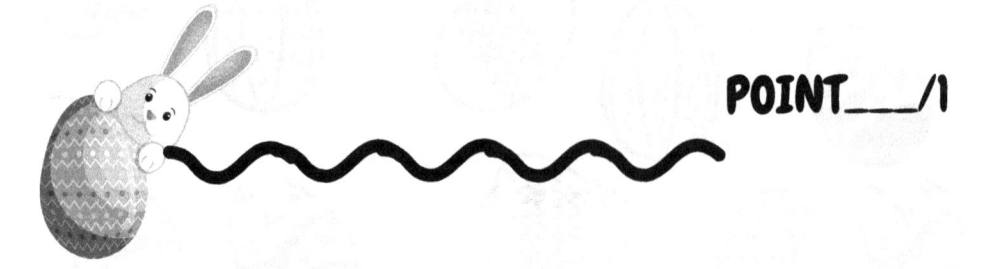

POINT____/1

Would yourather have your favorite athlete send you an Easter basket
or
your favorite TV/movie star? (And who would it be?)

POINT____/1

PLAYER 2

(DON'T FORGET TO EXPLAIN YOUR ANSWERS!)

Would you rather meet a friendly monster
or
a monster who's looking for friends?

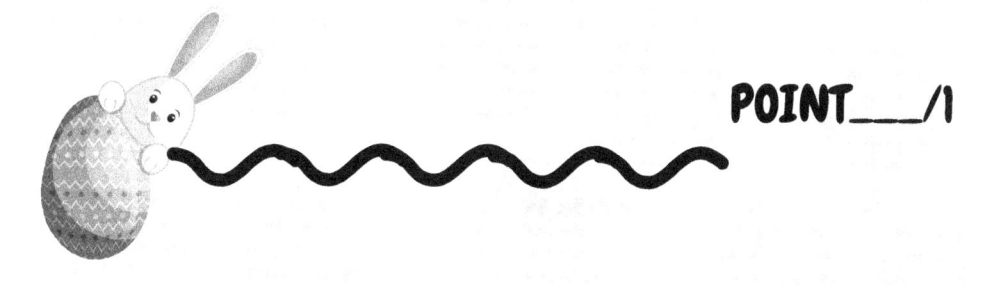

POINT___/1

Would you rather be in a food fight
or
just watch a food fight?

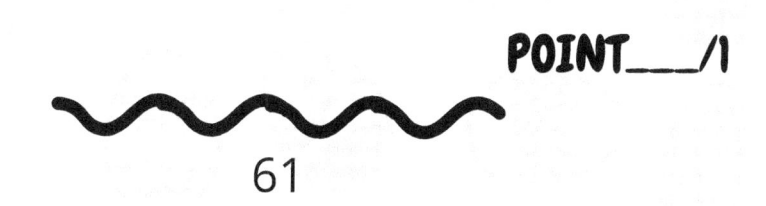

POINT___/1

PLAYER 1 POINT___/4

PLAYER 2 POINT___/4

ROUND 8

PLAYER 1

(DON'T FORGET TO EXPLAIN YOUR ANSWERS!)

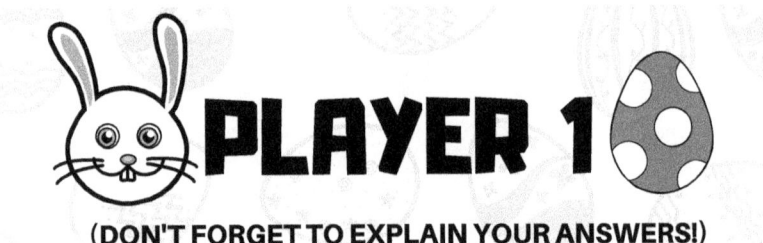

Would you rather be gossiped about by your classmates about what you did while on Spring Break
or
have them not remember whom you are?

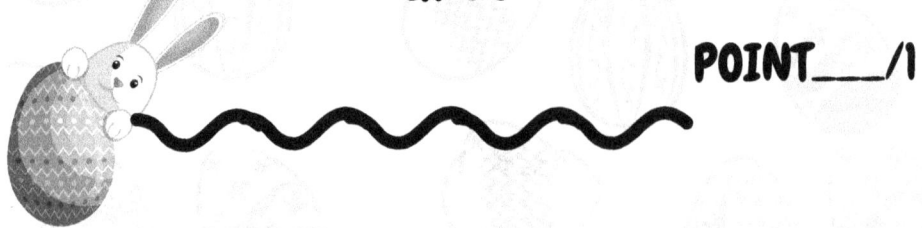

POINT___/1

Would you rather meet a friendly dinosaur
or
meet a friendly dragon?

POINT___/1

PLAYER 1

(DON'T FORGET TO EXPLAIN YOUR ANSWERS!)

Would you rather have to hide 500 plastic eggs
or
dye 500 hard boiled eggs?

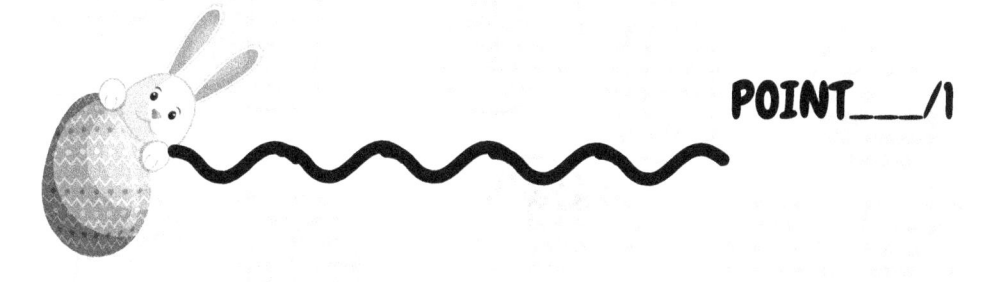

POINT___/1

Would you rather keep your money with Dad
or
Mom?

POINT___/1

PLAYER 2
(DON'T FORGET TO EXPLAIN YOUR ANSWERS!)

Would you rather have a unicorn of your own
or
be a unicorn?

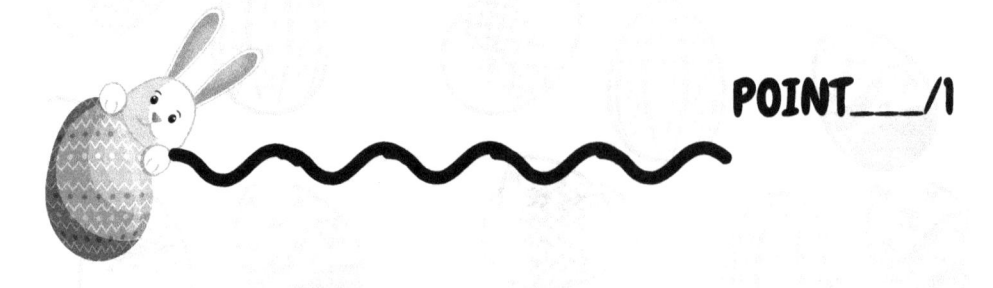

POINT____/1

Would you rather have a rabbit's ears
or
a rabbit's teeth?

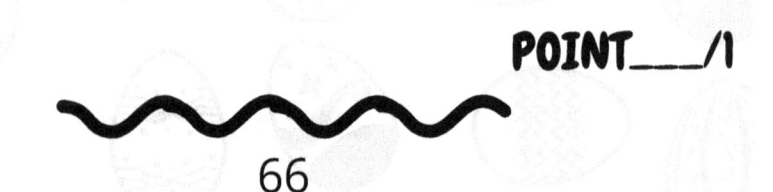

POINT____/1

PLAYER 2

(DON'T FORGET TO EXPLAIN YOUR ANSWERS!)

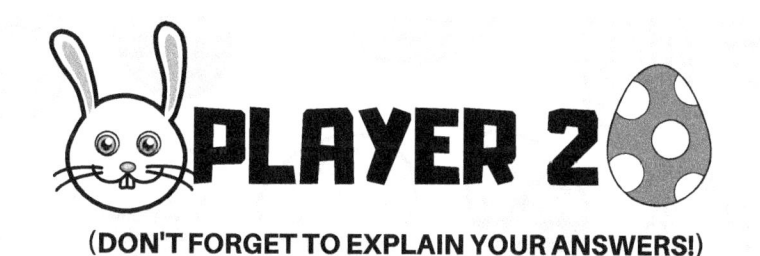

Would you rather have to live this Easter over and over in the coming year
or
give up talking to your friends and family for the next 6 months?

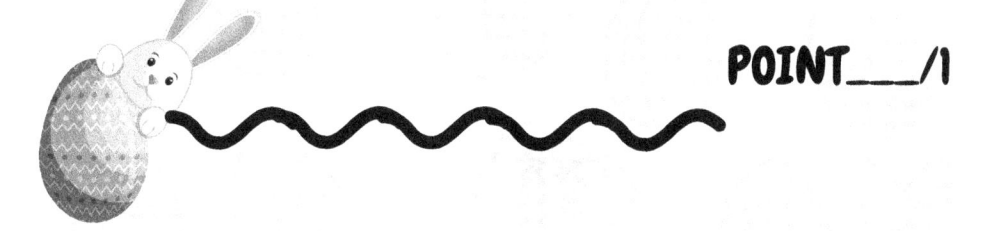

POINT___/1

Would you rather have no eyebrows or have pink eyebrows?

POINT___/1

PLAYER 1 POINT___/4

PLAYER 2 POINT___/4

ROUND 9

PLAYER 1

(DON'T FORGET TO EXPLAIN YOUR ANSWERS!)

Would you rather have to sing a spring song about baby chicks in front of your whole school
or
recite a heart-felt poem about baby chicks on a YouTube (where it would live for forever!)?

POINT___/1

Would you rather have to poop every hour
or
have to pee every hour?

POINT___/1

PLAYER 1

(DON'T FORGET TO EXPLAIN YOUR ANSWERS!)

Would you rather have really long fingernails
or
really long toenails?

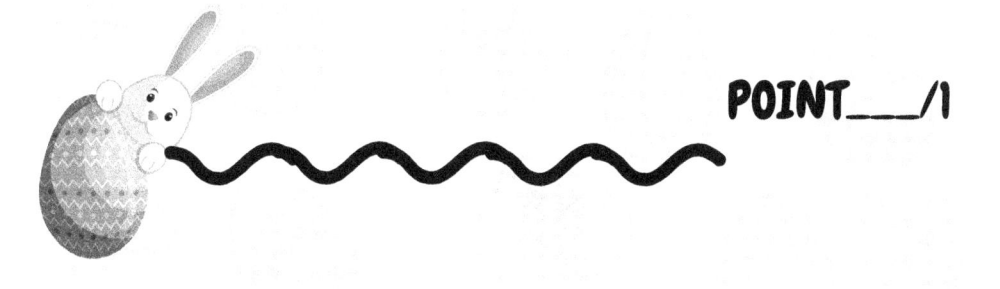

POINT___/1

Would you rather have a really scary smile
or
have a really loud laugh?

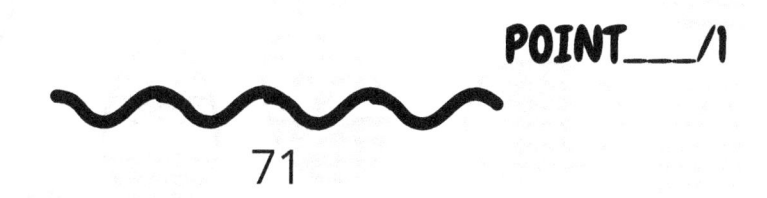

POINT___/1

PLAYER 2

(DON'T FORGET TO EXPLAIN YOUR ANSWERS!)

Would you rather not be able to taste anything
or
not be able to smell anything?

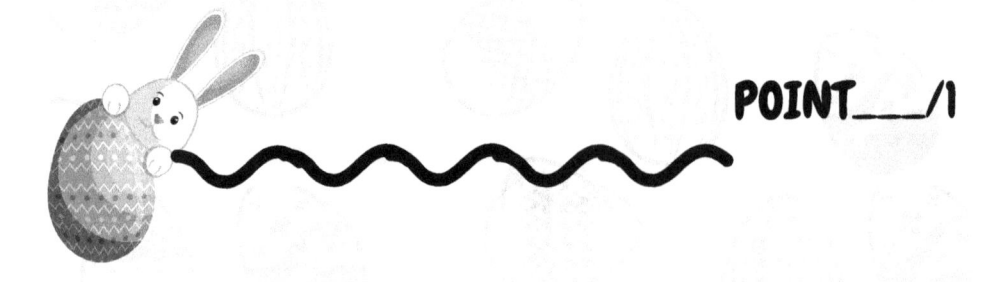

POINT____/1

Would you rather brush your teeth with ketchup
or
brush your teeth with hot sauce?

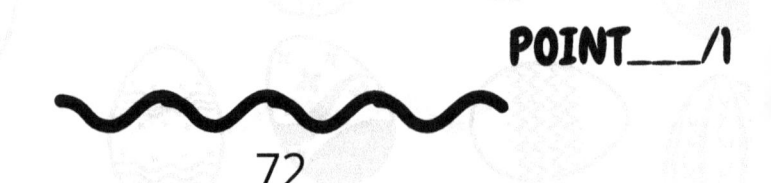

POINT____/1

PLAYER 2

(DON'T FORGET TO EXPLAIN YOUR ANSWERS!)

Would you rather have green eyes or yellow eyes?

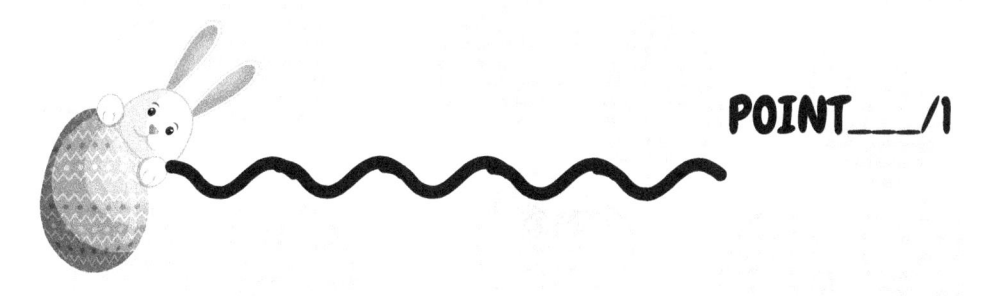

POINT___/1

Would you rather be a clown or meet a clown?

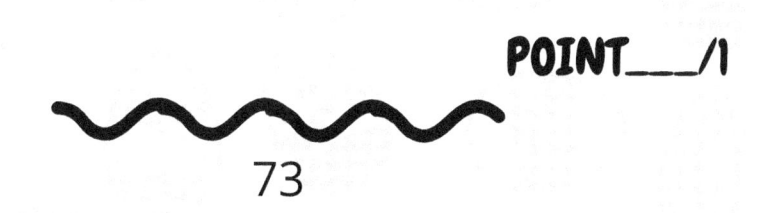

POINT___/1

PLAYER 1 POINT___/4

PLAYER 2 POINT___/4

ROUND 10

PLAYER 1

(DON'T FORGET TO EXPLAIN YOUR ANSWERS!)

Would you Plastic green grass for hair
or
large plastic egg for a body?

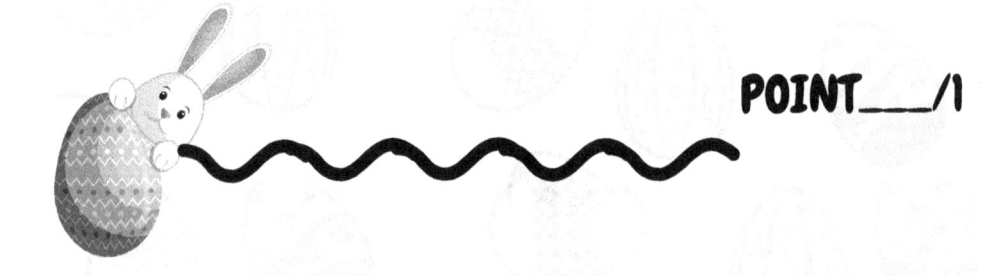

POINT____/1

Would you Search for 100 quarters in 500 eggs
or
50 dollar bills in 1,000 eggs in 5 minutes?

POINT____/1

PLAYER 1

(DON'T FORGET TO EXPLAIN YOUR ANSWERS!)

Would you Wings like a butterfly
or
feet like a rabbit?

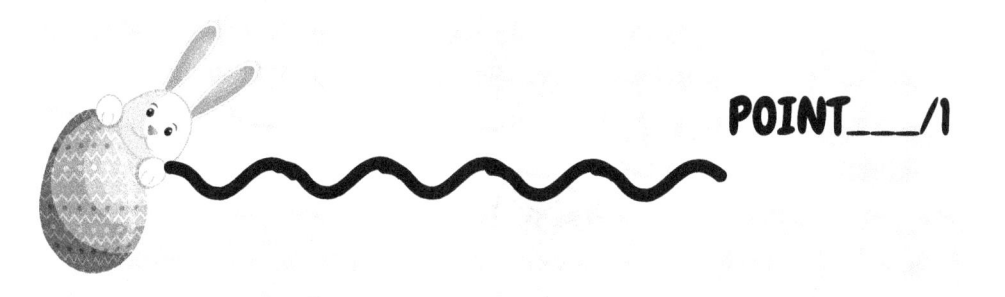

POINT___/1

Would you find hidden eggs?
or
Hide plastic eggs for friends

POINT___/1

PLAYER 2

(DON'T FORGET TO EXPLAIN YOUR ANSWERS!)

Would you Wear a basket for a hat
or
fancy bonnet for 1 week?

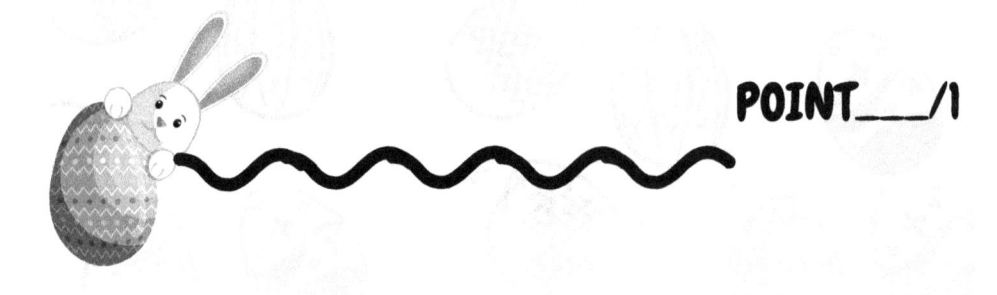

POINT___/1

Would you Carry an uncooked egg for
1 week everywhere you go
or
100 plastic eggs?

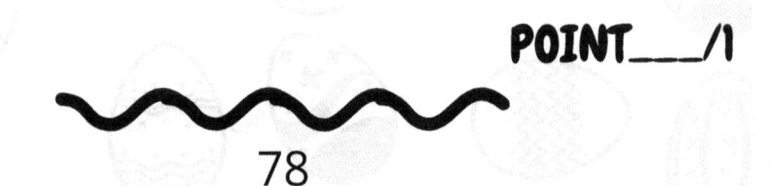

POINT___/1

PLAYER 2

(DON'T FORGET TO EXPLAIN YOUR ANSWERS!)

Would you Dress up as a bunny or Spring baby chick for 10 days?

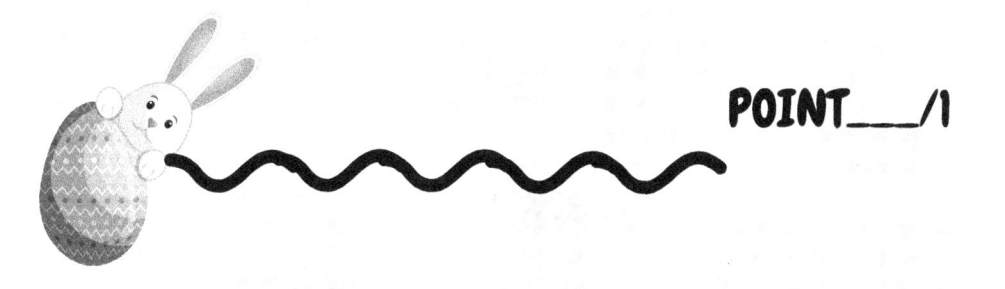

POINT___/1

Would you Basket filled with jelly beans or Chocolate bunnies?

POINT___/1

PLAYER 1 POINT___/4

PLAYER 2 POINT___/4

ROUND 11

PLAYER 1

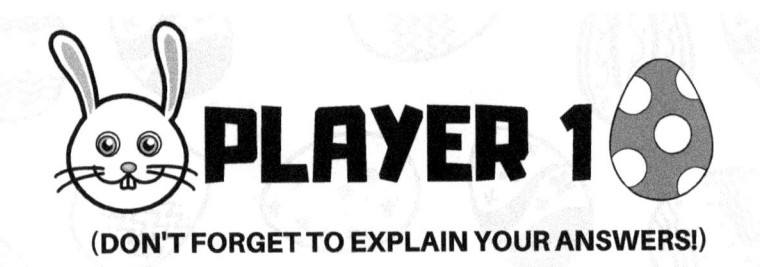

(DON'T FORGET TO EXPLAIN YOUR ANSWERS!)

Would you Walk like a caterpillar or crawl like a ladybug?

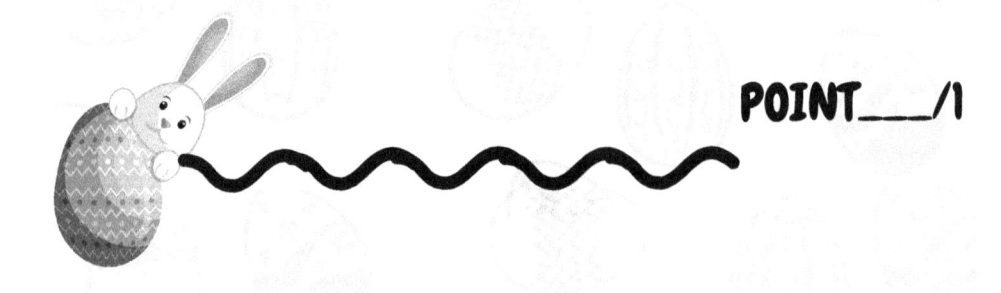

POINT___/1

Would you Bunny carrots (cheetos) or Bunny poop (chocolate covered raisins)

POINT___/1

PLAYER 1

(DON'T FORGET TO EXPLAIN YOUR ANSWERS!)

Make friends with a talking rabbit
or
a talking squirrel?

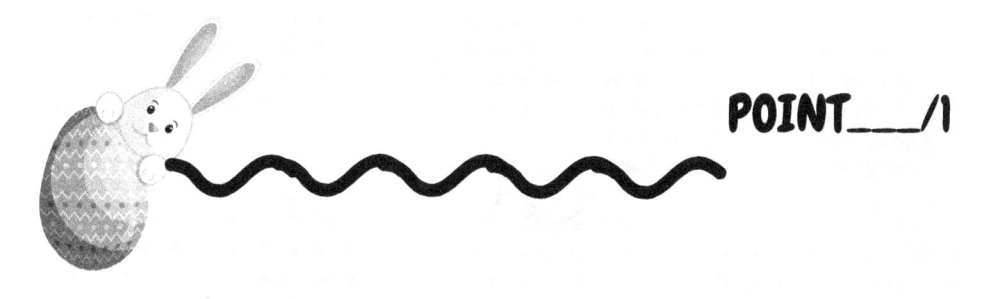

POINT___/1

Egg huntor
or
Scavenger hunt?

POINT___/1

PLAYER 2

(DON'T FORGET TO EXPLAIN YOUR ANSWERS!)

Would you Have a Peep marshmallow head
or
lamb legs?

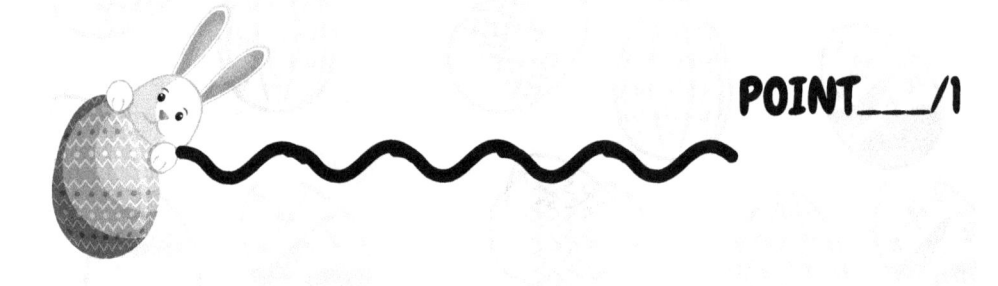

POINT____/1

Would you rather wake up with wings
or
wake up with a tail?

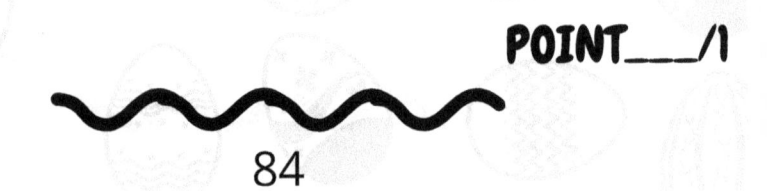

POINT____/1

PLAYER 2

(DON'T FORGET TO EXPLAIN YOUR ANSWERS!)

Fly a large kite
or
roll down a large hill in a field of grass?

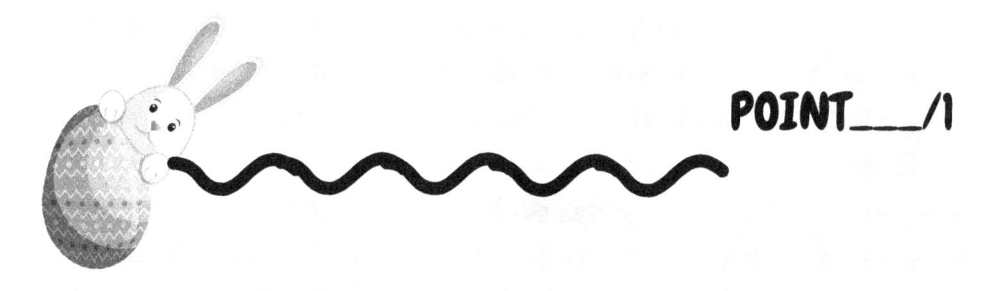

POINT___/1

Take care of wild rabbits
or
a bee hive?

POINT___/1

PLAYER 1 POINT___/4

PLAYER 2 POINT___/4

ROUND 12

PLAYER 1

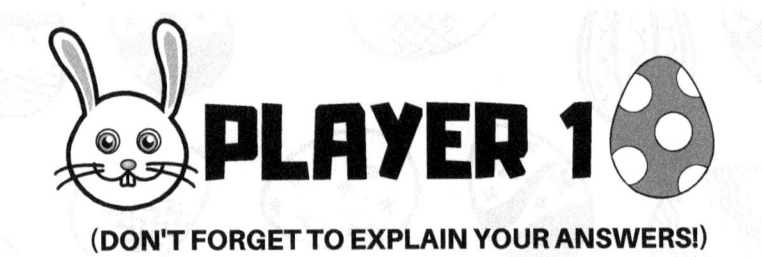

(DON'T FORGET TO EXPLAIN YOUR ANSWERS!)

Bright bold colors or pastels?

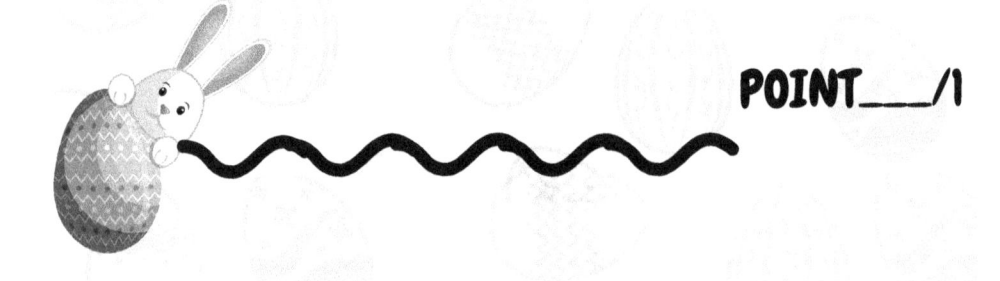

POINT___/1

Would you rather spend the day with the Easter Bunny or the Tooth Fairy?

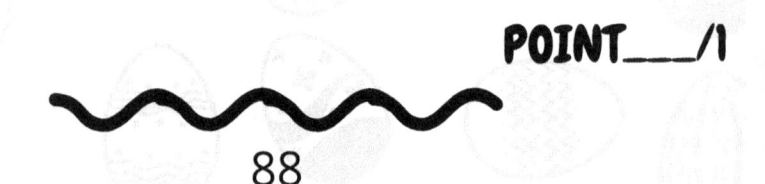

POINT___/1

PLAYER 1

(DON'T FORGET TO EXPLAIN YOUR ANSWERS!)

Would you rather hide the Easter eggs
or
hunt for the Easter eggs?

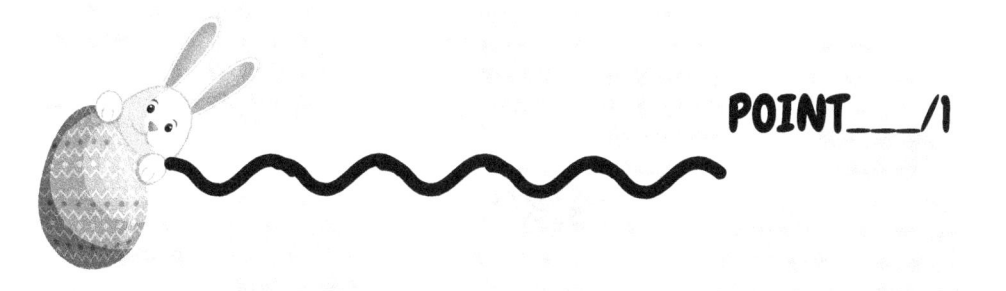

POINT___/1

Would you rather have a squeaky voice
or
a really loud voice?

POINT___/1

PLAYER 2
(DON'T FORGET TO EXPLAIN YOUR ANSWERS!)

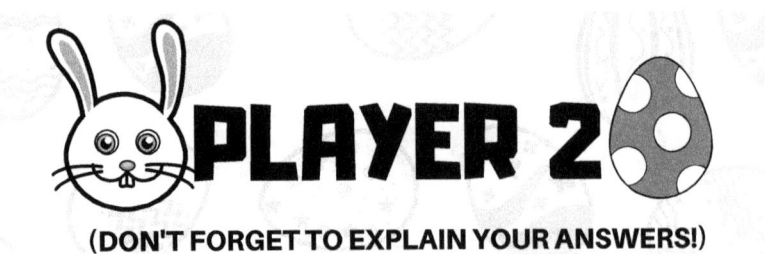

Color 100 Eggs or plant 2 trees?

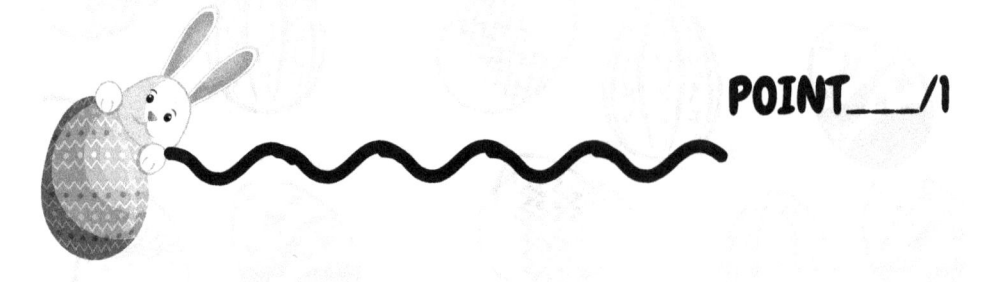

POINT___/1

Would you rather pee in a bucket or pee in a cup?

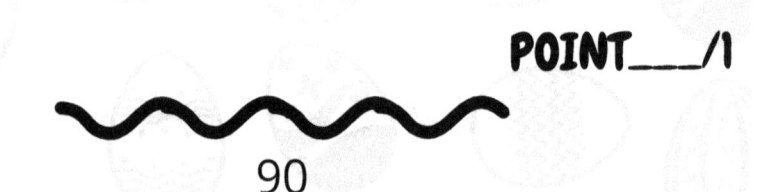

POINT___/1

PLAYER 2

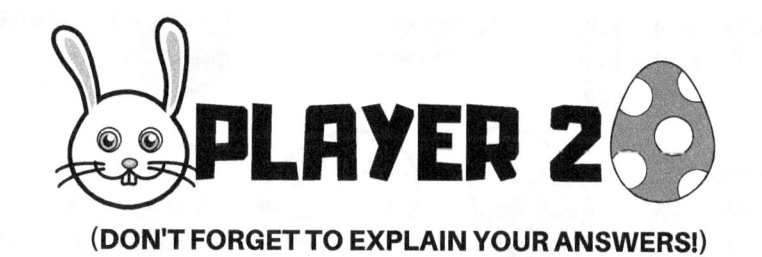

(DON'T FORGET TO EXPLAIN YOUR ANSWERS!)

Try to catch a squirrel or try to catch a frog?

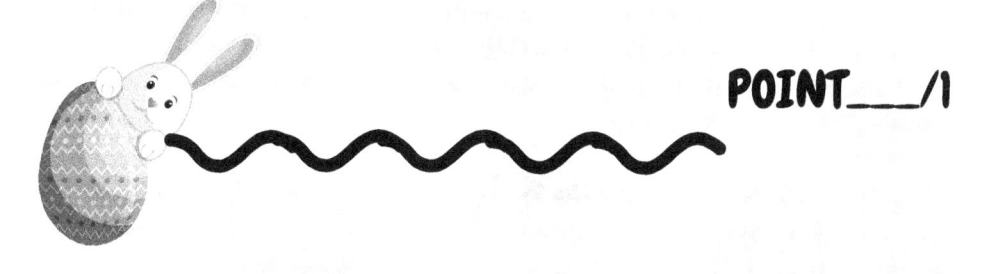

POINT____/1

Would you rather be pranked with a fake rat or a fake bug?

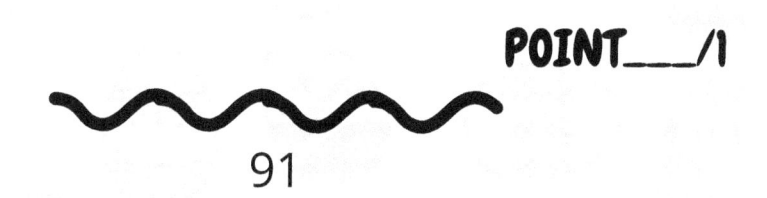

POINT____/1

PLAYER 1 POINT___/4

PLAYER 2 POINT___/4

ROUND 13

PLAYER 1

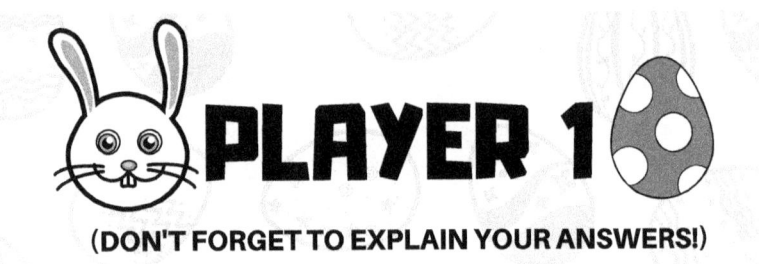

(DON'T FORGET TO EXPLAIN YOUR ANSWERS!)

Would you rather get cotton candy or get ice-cream at a park

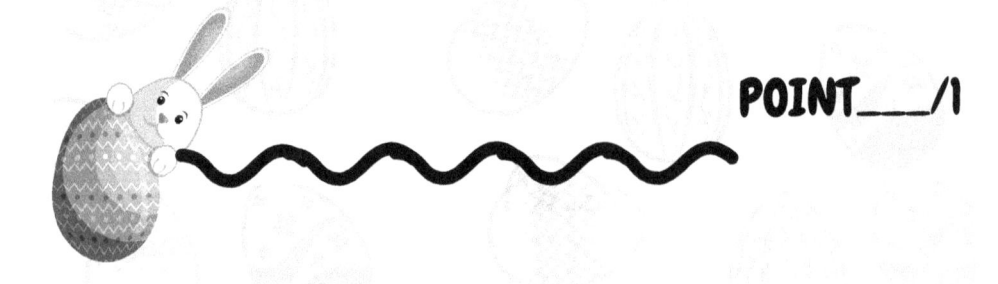

POINT___/1

Would you rather have only one close friend or lots of friends you're not too close to

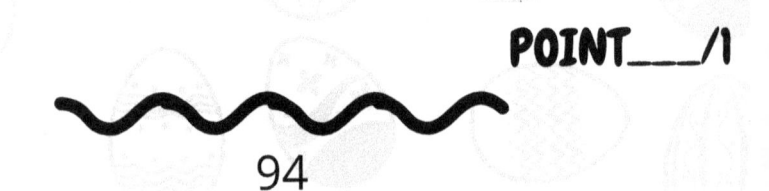

POINT___/1

PLAYER 1

(DON'T FORGET TO EXPLAIN YOUR ANSWERS!)

Would you rather go watch a circus show
or
be a part of a circus show

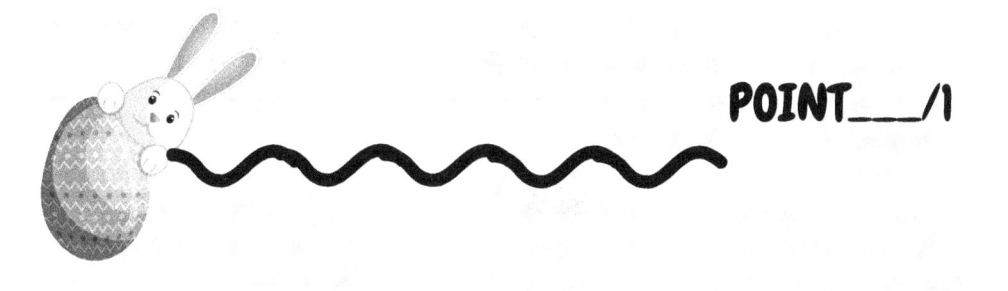

POINT___/1

Would you rather have a lot of superpowers for one week
or
just one superpower for a month

POINT___/1

PLAYER 2

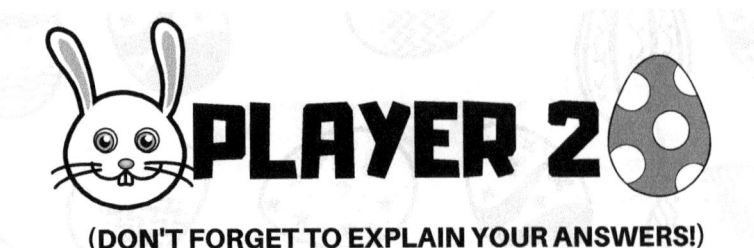

(DON'T FORGET TO EXPLAIN YOUR ANSWERS!)

Would you rather have large feet or large hands

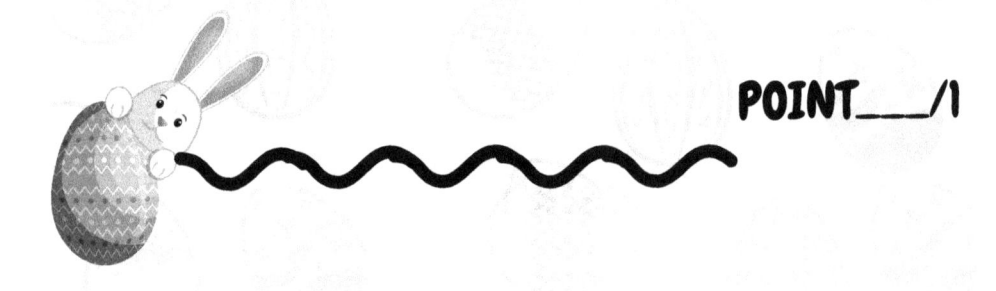

POINT___/1

Would you rather get a free boat cruise or a free plane ticket

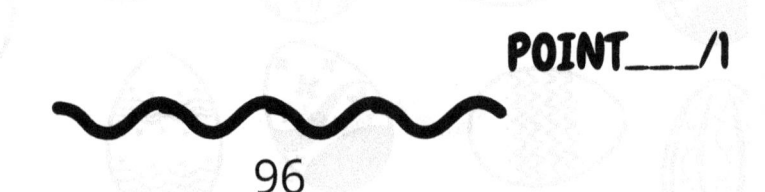

POINT___/1

PLAYER 2

(DON'T FORGET TO EXPLAIN YOUR ANSWERS!)

Would you rather have no friends or be surrounded by annoying people

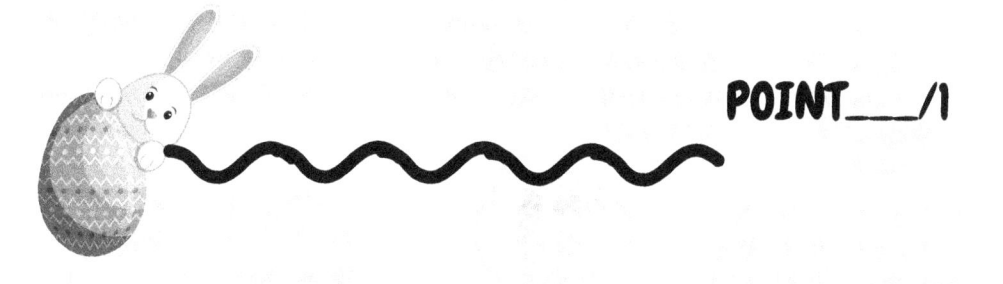

POINT___/1

Would you rather be feared by all or be liked by all

POINT___/1

PLAYER 1 POINT___/4

PLAYER 2 POINT___/4

ROUND 14

PLAYER 1

(DON'T FORGET TO EXPLAIN YOUR ANSWERS!)

Would you rather have no friends or be surrounded by annoying people

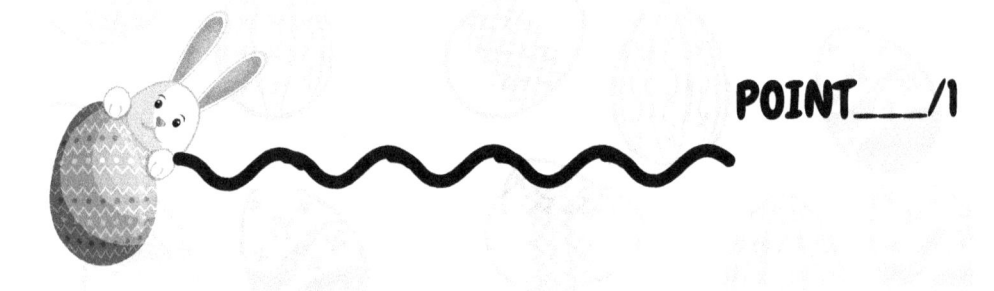

POINT___/1

Would you rather be feared by all or be liked by all

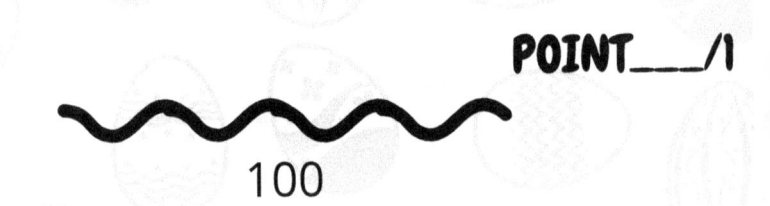

POINT___/1

PLAYER 1

(DON'T FORGET TO EXPLAIN YOUR ANSWERS!)

Would you rather get lots of hugs
or
lots of cuddles

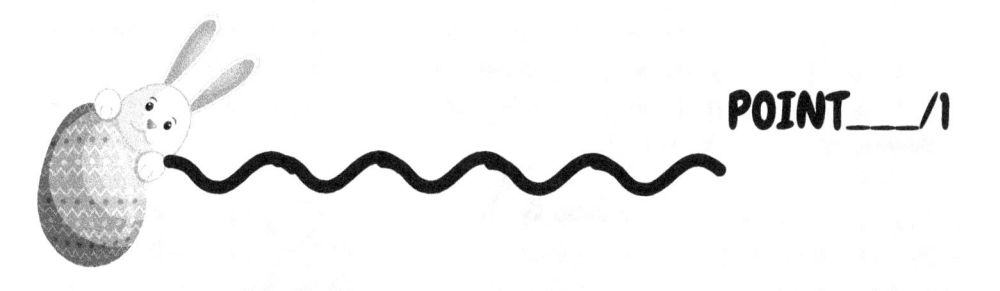

POINT___/1

Would you rather face your fears
or
forget you have fears

POINT___/1

PLAYER 2

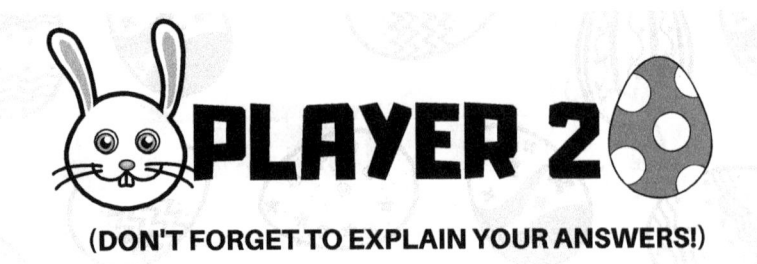

(DON'T FORGET TO EXPLAIN YOUR ANSWERS!)

Would you rather meet an Easter bunny
or
find lots of Easter eggs

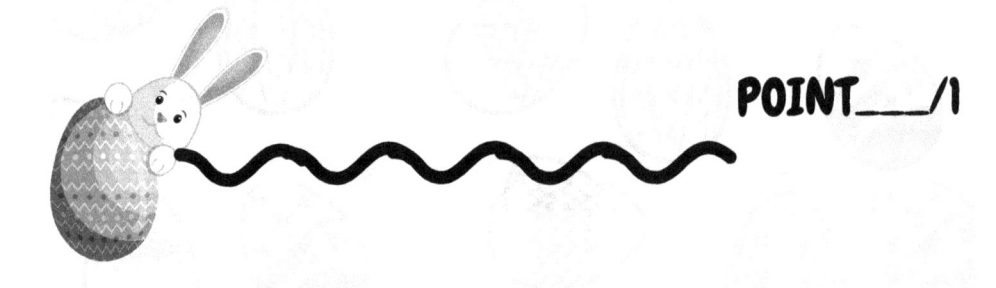

POINT____/1

Would you rather use glasses
or
get contact lenses?

POINT____/1

PLAYER 2

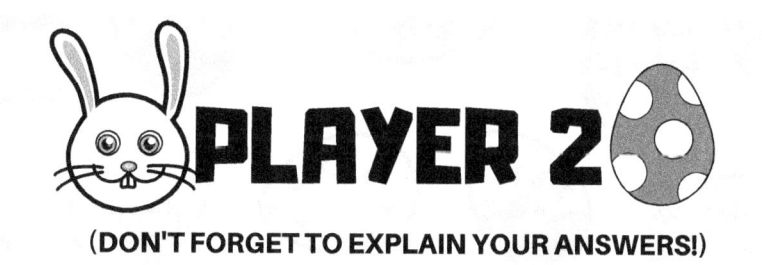

(DON'T FORGET TO EXPLAIN YOUR ANSWERS!)

Would you rather sleep beside a skunk or sleep beside a pig?

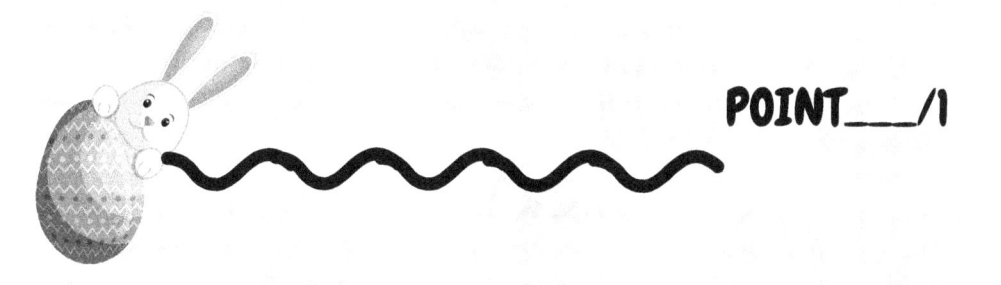

POINT___/1

Would you rather live in a world full of zombies or a world full of aliens?

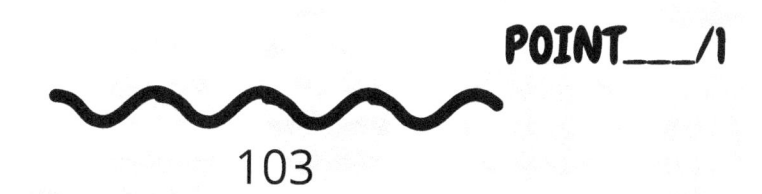

POINT___/1

PLAYER 1 POINT___/4

PLAYER 2 POINT___/4

ROUND 15

PLAYER 1

(DON'T FORGET TO EXPLAIN YOUR ANSWERS!)

Would you rather have blue skin like an alien
or
really white skin?

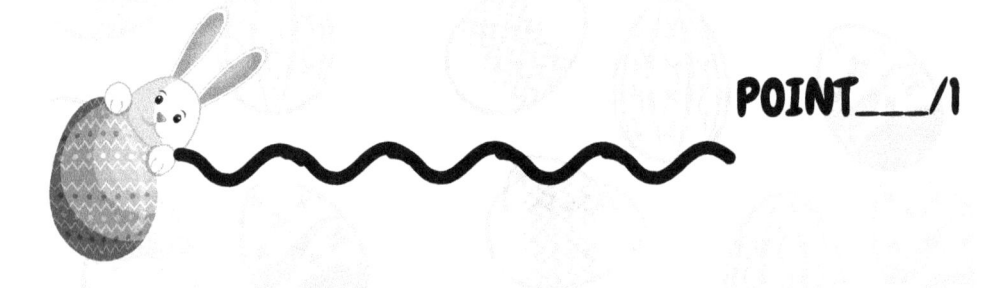

POINT___/1

Would you rather live in the sky permanently
or
live underwater permanently?

POINT___/1

PLAYER 1

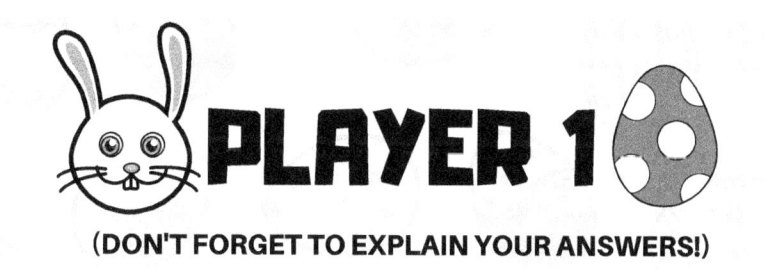

(DON'T FORGET TO EXPLAIN YOUR ANSWERS!)

Would you rather get into a fight with ducks
or
get chased by ducks?

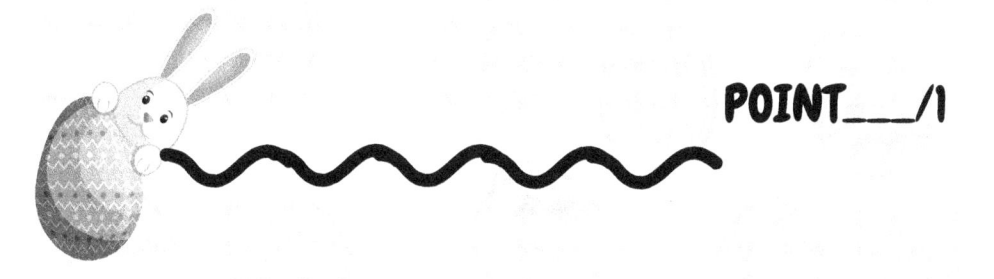

POINT___/1

Would you rather have a squeaky voice
or
a really loud voice?

POINT___/1

PLAYER 2

(DON'T FORGET TO EXPLAIN YOUR ANSWERS!)

Flowers for hair
or
Rain for eyelashes?

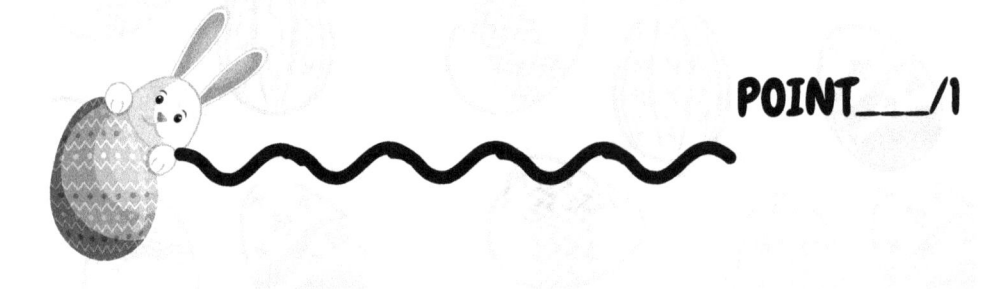

POINT___/1

Would you rather dance like a chicken in front of your friends
or
dance like a chicken on the internet?

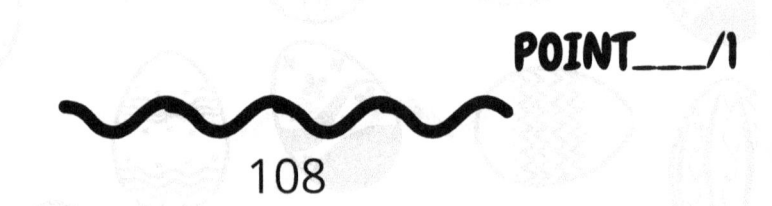

POINT___/1

PLAYER 2

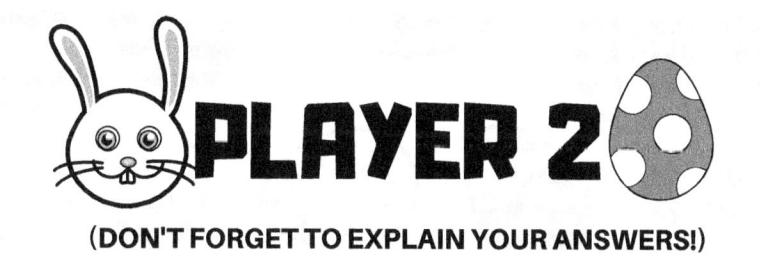

(DON'T FORGET TO EXPLAIN YOUR ANSWERS!)

Would you rather have multicolored hair or hair that tastes like candy?

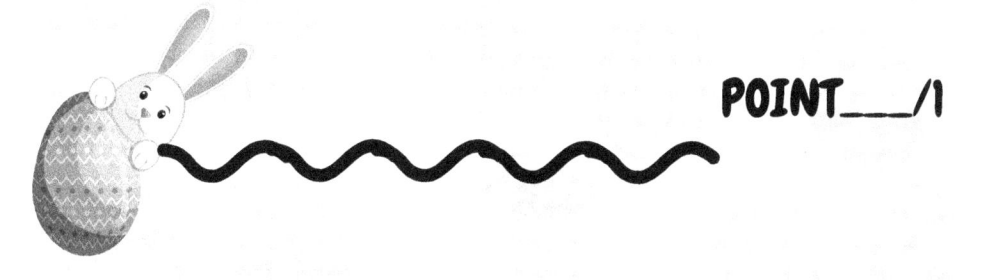

POINT___/1

Unicorns or Pegasus?

POINT___/1

PLAYER 2

(DON'T FORGET TO EXPLAIN YOUR ANSWERS!)

Would you rather have multicolored hair or hair that tastes like candy?

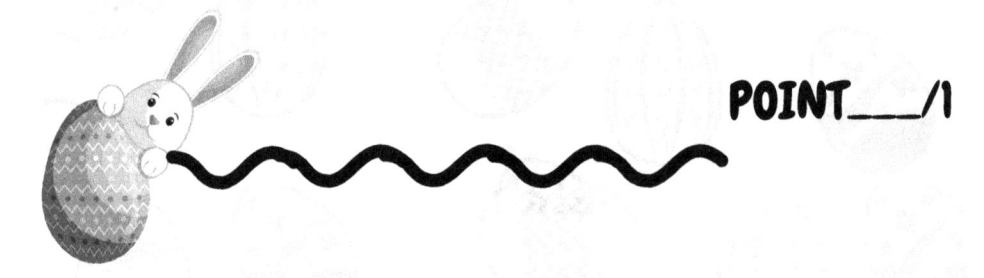

POINT___/1

Unicorns or Pegasus?

POINT___/1

PLAYER 1 POINT___/4

PLAYER 2 POINT___/4